Wakefield Press

Marra

Nicholas Newland, AM, was born in Adelaide in 1948 and is a fifth generation South Australian. His interest in the five sons of Simpson was ignited by his wanting to find out more about his grandfather, the youngest of the sons of Simpson and Jane Newland. His research uncovered more than he expected. Ironically he found out relatively little about his grandfather but a great deal about his grandfather's brothers. All Simpson and Jane's children were brought up in the Victorian era, where, in their parents' eyes, men were expected to be men – hence the title. The name 'Marra' remains obscure though it has been used several times by various Newland families over succeeding generations. It is of some comfort that some things remain secrets; we don't need to know everything!

Nicholas and his wife Suzanne have four sons between them, all of whom, along with siblings and cousins, will learn something of their antecedents from this book.

Marra

The making of men

NICHOLAS NEWLAND

Wakefield Press
16 Rose Street
Mile End
South Australia 5031
wakefieldpress.com.au

First published 2020

Cover design by Michael Deves, Wakefield Press
Edited by Penelope Curtin
Typeset by Michael Deves, Wakefield Press

ISBN 978 1 74305 705 6

A catalogue record for this book is available from the National Library of Australia

Wakefield Press thanks Coriole Vineyards for continued support

Contents

All photographs are from the Newland family archives unless stated otherwise.

Foreword

The privilege of writing the foreword to *Marra: The making of men* has fallen to us as a consequence of our knowing the author and our links with Simpson Newland, CMG, through my grandfather Alfred Allen Simpson, ironically, no blood relation. He bought Simpson Newland's house, Undelcarra, in 1918 from the proceeds of a happy speculation on wheat futures.

Although forty years apart in age, they would have been well acquainted, certainly through the Royal Geographical Society of Australasia, South Australian Branch (RGSSA), then a driving force for advancing exploration and scientific knowledge and supported by the great and the good.[1] Simpson Newland was the president between 1895 and 1900; he was also a pioneer, explorer, politician and author of the classic Victorian novel *Paving the Way*, written it is believed in the smoking room of Undelcarra.

Allen Simpson was President of the RGSSA between 1925 and 1930; its history describes him as the first of a succession of forward-looking presidents and 'intellectually one of its more adventurous'. He saw the need to hasten the mapping of the country using the aeroplane and supported both Madigan's exploration in Central Australia, leading to the naming of the

Simpson Desert, and Mawson's work in Antarctica, leading to the naming of Cape Simpson.

Coincidentally, the author of this book and his father were also subsequent presidents, continuing a family connection. This book, as much as anything else, describes how Simpson Newland and his wife Jane, both covertly and overtly, wanted to ensure that their five sons were brought up to be 'men'. This is not to suggest that they were chauvinistic; rather they were resilient and tough South Australians, to the extent that they achieved extraordinary things, some of which are recounted in this book.

The house that their father Simpson Newland bought in 1876 was already in its second iteration. It began as three creek-washed stone cottages on the bank of Second Creek in Adelaide and became a single-storey villa with a detached kitchen after its purchase by Robert Debney in 1852, who named it The Laurels. Debney was a successful cabinet-maker, supplying the joinery to the old Parliament House on North Terrace, Adelaide. He planted the introduced trees that now define the structure of the current Undelcarra garden.[2] An attractive painting of this house when Debney owned it was executed by Shaw in 1865 and is now in the Burnside Council Chambers.

Simpson Newland purchased The Laurels in 1876 and renamed it Undelcarra, a significant change in language. He noted the name as an Aboriginal word meaning 'under the hill' and made reference to a striking rock formation of the same name on his extensive pastoral property Marra, on the Darling River in New South Wales. That name has been used subsequently several times for both people and property. As such, it is fitting that it forms a principal part of the title of this book.

A number of insights into Simpson Newland's character can be drawn from his approach to the house rebuilding, which, I suggest, influenced his upbringing of his five children, all sons. He saw The Laurels as both old and small and seems to have set about its transformation with vigour, by doubling the number of rooms from ten to twenty and adding a second storey. He was innovative: inside was a light well, at the top of which were windows that opened to allow hot air to escape, while in the garden were storage tanks and 'pipes connected all over the grounds'. Because they were gravity-fed, they were of large diameter and were connected to solid brass taps, fittings that were still seen in the 1960s.

His and, one assumes, his wife's views on rearing these five sons are evident in his writings in *Memoirs of Simpson Newland CMG*:

> There was plenty of room for outdoor games and exercise, also timber and water to develop their propensities for work. As they grew older, horses, ponies and vehicles were at their disposal, and the training they received then fitted them to be self reliant in their boyhood and capable in their manhood. I have never believed in pampering of boys: if my sons wanted to ride, they caught their own ponies in the paddocks, and rode them bareback to the stables; if they desired more pocket money, they earned it by doing odd jobs on the place. I learnt my own lessons of life in a hard school. And it was my desire that my boys should learn that pleasures must be won and so foster in them a sense of responsibility, too often lacking, I fear, when life is made easy for the rising generation.

A curiosity that we found under the floorboards of the house was a number of unopened BHP annual reports, dated 1890 and addressed to Newland; whether their unread state contains an insight about his character is a matter for speculation.

We gain satisfaction from the thought that where we now live – as did our sons – is the place where these five sons grew up to be men worthy of mention. Perhaps some of the values of Simpson Newland, this formidable pioneer, were passed on to our sons as well. What follows is the story of his five sons, told by Nicholas Newland, AM, a great grandson.

We are most pleased to have provided this foreword.

Antony and Mary Lou Simpson

Introduction

This book has come into existence by chance. My original intention had been to find out something about my paternal grandfather Ralph Dimock Newland, who died relatively young, on 25 September 1933, at fifty-three years of age. He was the youngest of the five sons of Simpson Newland, CMG, and his wife Jane Isabella (1851–1939). Simpson had a half-brother Watts, whose descendants also live in South Australia and in other parts of Australia. Lack of time, space and knowledge has meant that they get little mention in this account, although some day someone may tell their story.

I own five pieces of memorabilia about Ralph: a childhood storybook (more concerned with the parents of Ralph's first wife, the Creswells, than the Newlands), a beautiful silver and ruby-red glass claret decanter, which was once part of a set, with six matching glasses. It was the prize awarded to Ralph in 1896 as the winner of the half-mile at St Peter's College and it was passed on to me by my long-dead father, Basil Creswell Newland. I also have a bible given to Ralph by his mother Jane Isabella Newland (née Layton) in 1914; a tattered photograph album started by Ralph in 1904 containing a variety of photos, many from South Africa; and an 1899 photograph of him as a player in the Iroquois Lacrosse Club team. Aside from these mementos, I know that he was trained as an industrial chemist and he worked in gold mines in South Africa, before returning to South Australia before the First World War, initially as a sheep farmer and later as a viticulturist. His later life was not a happy one. He is understood to have been in failing health as a result of his work in the mining industry and his death certificate records the cause of death as cirrhosis of the liver and chronic nephritis. There is no known suggestion that he was an alcoholic – although research for this book has unearthed other various surprises.

As this research continued, it became very apparent that there was much to say about all five brothers, given the extensive family records on the first and third brothers. However, for Ralph, the original object of my quest, information has largely been gleaned by researching his four elder brothers, particularly his first brother Henry Simpson and his third brother Victor Marra.

The apparent unwillingness on the part of my father to talk about his family is intriguing and perplexing. It was quite clear to my sisters and me that our father was very interested in world and natural history, the nature of people and the communities they inhabit, and the fortunes of South Australia. While his father Ralph was the principal reason for this book, the relative lack of information available on him means that his presence in this book is minimal. By a stroke of luck, it was my attempts to find out something of this 'shadowy figure', a description used by my father's deceased younger brother Dr Malcolm Creswell Newland about his father Ralph, that led to my discovery of so much privately held and therefore previously unseen material. In some ways Ralph's third brother Victor Marra Newland has become this book's principal character – he was an adventurer and soldier with an extraordinary and remarkably full life, the details of which have remained largely unknown until now. As Victor Newland spent time in Africa, arriving before his younger brother Ralph, I have been able, through his letters and other material, to learn much about Victor and something about my paternal grandfather Ralph.

My three sisters and I were brought up in Adelaide by parents from families that had each in their own way made an undoubted contribution to the South Australian community. Coincidentally, these families had a common link with the Wyatt Benevolent Trust, of which my maternal grandfather, Henry Howard Austin, was secretary for fifty-three years, from 1893 to 1946. My great grandfather Simpson Newland, CMG, was president of the board of that trust from 1900 to 1925 and his son, Sir Henry Simpson Newland, became a trustee in 1928 and was chairman from 1950 to 1966. His place was then taken by his son Ridgeway, first as a trustee, and later chairman, from 1982 to 1985. This trust is still going strong, although no family members are now involved.

As a young boy, I recall my sisters and I being taken by my parents to meet Sir Henry, or Uncle Hal, as we called him, when he was in his late eighties. He was quite deaf and somewhat intimidating to us children. Over subsequent years, I discovered more about him and some of his idiosyncrasies, which I think endeared him to some and infuriated others. For reasons that remain a mystery to me, my father and his two brothers spoke little about either Sir Henry or his four younger brothers. All five sons of Simpson and Jane had interesting lives, despite two of them suffering tragic deaths at relatively young ages. In the past I have wondered whether these events were just too painful for the subsequent generation to pass on details on these earlier family members. By the same token, why would the notable achievements of that previous generation of Newland men, including quite remarkable achievements during their lives, be kept hidden?

My initial attempts to elicit information on Ralph Newland also occurred by chance. My father's younger brother Malcolm lived the last few years of his life alone and quite close to where my family and I live, in an inner Adelaide suburb. As I said earlier, I was keen to find out more about the early life of my father, which I knew had been a difficult one. He had been born a cripple and his mother Hazel (née Creswell) had died two to three weeks after the birth of Malcolm, Ralph's youngest son, when Ralph was thirty-two and my father was three years old. Ralph's three sons, John, Basil (my father) and Malcolm, were bundled off to boarding school, initially to Queen's School in North Adelaide and then to St Peter's College in Adelaide, at a young age. They did not receive the sort of parental support that most other children would have had, which may in part explain why my sisters, cousins and I were told so little about our paternal grandparents.

It has occurred to me that perhaps my father felt there was little to tell about Ralph by comparison with his elder brothers, particularly Henry, Philip and Victor. As this book will reveal, each of these men in their own way had experiences that are astonishing and extraordinary in their breadth, experiences that are likely to have had an influence in moulding their personalities. Henry was clearly a clever and skilled person in a developing field of surgery, especially plastic surgery, and Philip was a sportsman of great skill. Victor was more an adventurer, possessing what today would be described as the ultimate 'can do' attitude. Clive aspired to be a successful country doctor, and Ralph appeared to want to be a pastoralist like his father before him. A common thread is that all five were undoubtedly courageous and possessed a strong sense of striving to achieve their best for king and country, irrespective of the odds and risks.

Both Philip and Clive died in mid-life and, as with Ralph, the passage of time and the lack of accessible information make it hard to judge the characters and personalities of these three sons. My research indicates that their father Simpson Newland was undoubtedly tough and uncompromising, and, along with his wife Jane, clearly expected all five of his sons to emulate and probably to promote the 'manly' characteristics he clearly believed in and that he himself, with support from his wife, had developed and had put into action.

Thanks to extensive records, in particular for Henry and Victor, held by family relatives and the State Library of South Australia, it has been possible to collate the information that has become the basis of the true stories and events in this book. It is a pity that the personalities of the brothers Philip, Clive and Ralph remain partially obscured by a relative lack of information. Perhaps the publication of this book will uncover clues that help to answer the question of whether these other brothers did indeed live up to their father's 'manly' expectations. After all, through this research I have discovered that son number four, Clive, was Simpson's favourite and that his tragic and violent accidental death at forty-one years was a bitter blow to him.

I find it intriguing that the gravestone for Ralph in the family plot at the Victor Harbor cemetery in South Australia has spelled his second name as 'Dimmock' and includes the following words: 'youngest son of Simpson Newland'. It could be the case that whoever chose the wording on this gravestone for the youngest son wanted, among other things, to have his second name spelled as for his English ancestors and to ensure his relationship with his father was made explicit. I suspect it was his mother Jane; however, this may be speculation on my part.

Ironically, two family generations after these men's deaths, their descendants, my cousins, all now in the latter part of their lives, along with my sisters and me, are interested in discovering what their respective grandfathers were really like. I had never spoken to any descendants of Philip or Clive until I was over sixty-five years old. Yet, without exception, when I approached these cousins out of the blue, they were universally agreed that we, as their descendants, should make the effort to place on the public record something about these ancestors of ours, for all of our sakes, our children and the wider community. For my part, and I suspect much the same applies to my sisters and my cousins, if we do not make this effort now, this detailed information, apart from that held in the State Library, may well be lost, possibly for ever. While there is some interest from our respective children, it is not enough to guarantee that this extraordinary story, particularly about the third generation of Newlands will be researched, let alone recorded and made available in the public arena.

I also believe that it is much more difficult for the generations following mine to appreciate that there is a real, largely untold, story about these predecessors of ours. Life in Victorian Australia and later years is interesting and relevant to many, and in the case of the Newland family particularly to South Australians. Furthermore, the story of Simpson's five sons may well help those of us who are descendants to understand more about our respective parents' lives. The recounting of the deeds and circumstances of these men does not imply that they were 'better' than others; it is merely intended to add to the record of early life in the growing community of South Australia, and at the same time fill in gaps for my generation, who may question why our parents were the way they were, and indeed even account for the characteristics of the following generation of Newlands. My siblings, cousins and I acknowledge that we believe this narrative to be important to the South Australian community; others may disagree. I, as author of this account, hope this is not the case.

I would like to acknowledge the help I have received from my younger sister Rebecca and later my elder sister Rosalind, both of whom made transcribing letters held by the family and in the State Library of South Australia so much easier. Rosalind also took on the unenviable task of editing an early draft. I want to acknowledge especially my second cousin Leonie Matheson (née Dutton), who has been most generous with access to the letters and other memorabilia given to her by her grandfather Victor Marra and which she has assiduously kept for many years. Other family members, including cousins Henry and John, have also been generous in providing a great deal of material, without which this account could not have been assembled.

1

South Australia: Historical context

This story begins with reflections on the social and physical context in which the sons of Simpson and Jane Newland found themselves as young men in the second half of the nineteenth century. Just as Simpson's father and mother forty years earlier had been affected by the prevailing social, economic, political and ideological conditions of the day, so were the three generations of Newlands discussed, to varying degrees, in this book. In the latter part of the nineteenth century, South Australia was a developing colony, one supposedly being established with utopian ideals, but one that was undergoing a difficult period of development; this was the society of which these Newland generations were part.

In Chapter II of the 1866 publication, *South Australia – its Progress and Prosperity* by A. Forster[3] the following magnanimous and probably inaccurate description of the colony of South Australia is given:

> The colony, as might be supposed from its immense extent, contains a great variety of soil and scenery. Extensive plains, comprising many millions of acres of arable land, and chiefly free of timber, extend from Aldinga in the south, to Mount Remarkable

> in the north. These plains are flanked on the eastern side by a mountain chain, of moderate elevation, running from north to south, with occasional breaks, for three hundred miles, and terminating at Cape Jervis … Beyond this range to the eastward and north-east, and before reaching the Murray scrub, the country is broken and hilly, with a good deal of timber, and a large extent of the finest agricultural land.

What a glowing description of a place which we now know would struggle to prosper and yet was being described in these terms a few years prior to the birth of Simpson and Jane's first son.

The first Newland arrived in South Australia in 1839. Ridgeway William Newland and family had to choose between making something out of the very little available after their arrival, or returning to something familiar, albeit less than attractive, in England. Ridgeway chose the former, which would not have been easy. As a religious Dissenter, he was not only leader of those many souls who accompanied him on the long and uncomfortable voyage in the ship *Sir Charles Forbes*, he also spurned the support of the established church in its various forms. At the suggestion of Governor George Gawler, he moved his family and flock away from Adelaide, where most of the population resided in the new colony of South Australia, to Encounter Bay, south of Adelaide. This locality became what is now known as Victor Harbor. In 2018 South Australians take for granted the hour or so drive down the Southern Expressway from Adelaide to Victor Harbor, but for Ridgeway and his followers on their first trip there was no established road and two relatively unknown Indigenous guides. Today most people would find the prospect of such a trip daunting, if not inconceivable. Various publications give descriptions of this 1839 trip, some of which are included in the next chapter of this book. One can only imagine the doubts and fears the participants in this expedition experienced. As for Ridgeway, his apparently unshakeable belief in himself, as well as the opportunity to make his mark on a community in his newly adopted country, meant that the risks were less worrying or confronting. The infant settlement of South Australia was initially fraught with problems, principally economic and social in nature, so it is not inconceivable that Ridgeway might have had some doubts. The colony of South Australia had been established with good intentions: no penal servitude; careful planning by its English founders, albeit from a distance of more than 12,000 miles; a land-investment strategy that was supposed to be self-funding; and a physical environment that was portrayed in the literature of the time and for the following couple of decades as being highly enticing. The author of the publication, *Early Experiences of Life in South Australia*, J.B. Bull[4], notes in the preface to the second edition that the South Australian Association had been founded by an Act of the Imperial Parliament of the United Kingdom. This Act specified, among other things, that no convicts should ever be sent to the colony and that the colony should be founded on the Wakefield Scheme, pending the granting of a Constitution by the Imperial Parliament once the population reached 50,000 souls.

Why would anyone hesitate to come here and bring a family to what some might describe as the promised land?

A later publication, the two-volume *The History of South Australia,* published in London,[5] describes the founding of the colony as:

> a story of protracted struggle against difficulties, of indomitable energy and perseverance, and of final success. The novelty of the scheme of colonization propounded, the untried character of the

> principles upon which it was proposed to establish the colony, the limited knowledge of the territory to be occupied combined to give the [Imperial] Parliament and the public an idea that the well-meaning projectors [*sic*] were visionaries and enthusiasts seeking to establish a Utopian settlement. Nevertheless the development of the scheme was watched with interest, even by those who did not believe it would issue in success; while the opposition of a few, who had the prosperity of other colonies at heart, only tended to give impetus to the labours of the fathers and founders of South Australia.

Ridgeway and family and followers could justifiably be counted among those fathers and founders.

The cold reality of little resembling 'civilisation' as might be hoped for; problems with lack of access to surveyed land, notwithstanding the honourable intentions of the first Surveyor-General Colonel William Light; an alien climate; strange vegetation; and the presence of the Aboriginal people were just a few of the issues to be appreciated by the newcomers upon their arrival after a sea voyage of several months. Most pioneers must have been frustrated and some were angered by what confronted them.

It is in this context that this story has its starting point. Yet this struggling community made some remarkable achievements in a relatively short space of time. The list includes the establishment of the first municipality in Australia (the city of Adelaide), the largest town hall in the Southern Hemisphere, the world-famous Torrens title land ownership system, women's suffrage, Ridley's stripper, free secondary education and a prominent role in planning Federation, as well as other 'firsts'. This was the socio-political setting in which Simpson and

Jane Newland and their family were lucky enough to establish themselves and to raise their sons.

There is little information to be found on Simpson's remarkable decision to leave his immediate family at Encounter Bay and in effect become a squatter at Marra station in the Riverina, along the Darling in New South Wales, although it is assumed that his move occurred somewhere between 1855 and 1860. My visit to the region in 2013 and a discussion with local historian Michael McInerney, living at Polocara station, near Tilpa (once part of Marra), revealed that several South Australians had made such a move to try their luck along this part of the Darling.

It can also be assumed that Simpson made a lot of money from his pastoral activities, although for many years life for him would have been tough. The later move back to Adelaide, in 1876, the purchase of what became Undelcarra, a mansion of considerable size, and over forty acres of land are some indication that he and Jane were not impoverished. He was also able to assist all of his children financially, although he had brought them up with the clear expectation that they were to make their own way in life. The sons' early lives at Undelcarra would have been reasonably privileged, with money, connections with South Australian society and a good education available to all of them. The relative comfort of their lives is described in the various chapters about the individual sons and is revealed through some of the photographs, including those of weddings. The family appeared to have easy access to the best Adelaide could offer.

It could be argued that some of the political issues of the time, such as the Northern Territory of South Australia and the most effective use of the Murray River, were not the easiest or possibly the most rewarding areas in which Simpson and his family became so involved. However, these were matters of great relevance and importance to South Australia towards the end of the nineteenth century, and many would argue that some still are. Also, Empire was still strong and things 'British' were, not surprisingly, strong influences in their lives.

Simpson and Jane's five children were born over a seven-year period, from 1873 to 1880, after Simpson had accumulated significant wealth as a pastoralist, largely through his own efforts on the Darling River in New South Wales. His time as a pastoralist was tough and lonely, and he took risks that a man who had married at a younger age may not – he married at the age of thirty-eight. His expectations of his children are a partial reflection of this period of his life, although both his parents appear to have had a profound influence on him as well, as this story attempts to show.

When his life at Undelcarra began, Simpson was concerned to achieve status in South Australian society, but in his family life he was committed to instilling self-reliance in his sons. Clearly, Simpson and Jane were well connected and they appeared not to be averse to participating fully in this largely colonial Adelaide-focused society. It is inevitable that their circumstances affected their sons in various ways. Adelaide at that time was still a relatively small place and it would have been far easier then to make a name for oneself than perhaps it is now. My research indicates that Simpson did not overtly seek 'fame and fortune', but he had views about many things and he was forthright in expressing some of those views in places where he surmised that they would be heard. As happens with controversial issues, some were accepted and some were not, meaning that inevitably he had his critics.

Irrespective of Simpson's critics, all of the sons did indeed make their own way in life, largely in accordance with parental expectations, although they would have been well aware that if circumstances became too grim, they had a fallback. While father Simpson was somewhat uncompromising and was similar in manner and behaviour to his own strict father, he was not ungenerous with his sons, and why not, since he had the resources? In the latter part of his life, he experienced more than his share of grief, losing two sons and a daughter-in-law. He also suffered a bad accident as an old man, being knocked down by a car when he was over seventy years old, which is somewhat ironic, given the risks he took when at Marra, as the story about him in Chapter 3 of this book shows.

What is behind the Marra name? Aside from its inclusion in the book's title, the name 'Marra' figures prominently in this account for several reasons, although the origin of the name is not certain. My research reveals that 'Marra' in the Kaurna (Adelaide region) language means 'hand', according to the *The Native Tribes of South Australia* (page 131), originally published in 1879 by E.S. Wigg and Sons and subsequently re-published by the Friends of the State Library of South Australia. Whether this meaning was the reason for the use of the name is not known.

I am gratified that the name endures in various forms today. Some properties in Australia in which the current generations of Newlands are involved still carry the name. It is the second name of one of Simpson's five sons, as well as of the third son of one of Clive's grandchildren, who is now aged well over sixty and living in Western Australia. It would be a good thing if the name survives into the future, but that depends on descendants being prepared to use it. Perhaps this book might encourage such use.

There is no better way to end this chapter than to quote two excerpts from *South Australia: Its history, resources, and productions* edited by W. Harcus, JP, and published in London in 1876,[6] midway in the period when Simpson and Jane's five sons were born. With fifteen chapters and nearly one hundred illustrations, most of which are designed to augment the book's text, the book is grandiose and extravagant in its claims about South Australia; for example, it refers to 'magnificent plains of agricultural land, mountain ranges stretching for hundreds of miles and often covered with large timber, chiefly eucalyptus, and lovely enchanting valleys through which in winter, creeks – in some instances deserving the name of rivers – run' (p. 18). Later on in the book the following appears (p. 145):

> Amongst the Colonies which are destined to greatness, I believe South Australia is in the foremost rank. She possesses most of the elements of expansion and progress. I know no Colony which presents greater attractions or gives a higher promise of success to careful, industrious, hopeful settlers than South Australia does. It has a magnificent and salubrious climate, a fruitful soil, an abundance of mineral wealth, millions of acres of unoccupied land inviting the industry of man.

How many South Australians today would second such notions?

2

In the beginning: The pioneer pastor

The lives of all of us are shaped by the people around us and the context in which live. We are invariably a product of these influences and many people are adept at using them to build character and personality. The men whose lives are the subject of this book were very much shaped by their situation at the time. Indeed, the underpinning influence of their parents and the values of those parents and of the generation before theirs surfaces time after time, with their stories strongly affected by their relationships with both parents and particularly their parents' reaction to leaving the familiarity of their country of birth – England – including their responses to travelling to what then would have been regarded as the other end of the earth. This was at a time when transport arrangements were basic, living conditions spartan and communication with the rest of the distant world sporadic, unreliable and often non-existent for long periods.

All good stories must have a beginning. This account of personalities all now long dead and the way they approached their lives has its roots in an unusual and clearly an exceptional person. Without a description of the Reverend Ridgeway William

Newland and the way he deliberately or inadvertently established a series of benchmarks for his children, this book would be an incomplete and meagre record. The decisions and actions of this man inevitably had an influence on subsequent generations.

In various places in this account, the spelling of the names of the protagonists is examined, the first of these being Ridgeway himself. While the historical record shows that he was christened and known in England as 'Ridgeway', for some unknown reason the 'e' in his first name seems to disappear when his name is recorded in South Australia. This account adopts his 'correct name' – Ridgeway – as that seems to be the intent of those who originally chose his name.

Ridgeway was born in 1790 at Well in Hampshire, England. He started his working life apprenticed to his watchmaker father and also worked in a mill. His decision to enter the Christian ministry in 1813 led to his becoming a student at Old College, Hoxton, in northeast London. The college's principal was a Dr Simpson, who apparently made a great impression on Ridgeway, to the extent that the Simpson name has remained through four subsequent generations of his descendants.

I use information from an article 'Old-time memories', written in 1895 by Simpson, the third of Ridgeway's sons and the subject of the next chapter, to illuminate the manner and substance of his father Ridgeway. The article was written when Simpson was over seventy years old and it can be assumed that the description he gives is reasonably objective. His relationship with his father Ridgeway appeared to be more than sound, and he had much admiration for him:

> among the relics yet remaining on the family archives is a painting of the principal, Dr Simpson, who has bequeathed

> his name to succeeding generations who have descended from his old pupil. Judging from the canvas the doctor must have possessed a stern strong face, and I can well believe that he stamped his powerful character in ineffaceable lines upon the more or less impressionable young student. Be this as it may, young Newland grew to manhood with all the unyielding convictions and indomitable resolutions that have ever marked the old Puritan sect of Independents to which he belonged. There could be no two paths to righteousness, no deviation to the right or to the left, no possibility of tempering or delaying when duty called, or as he conceived, the Divine will indicated, the course to be followed. For him, the line between the saint and the sinner was drawn with rigid distinctness; the one was the heir to never-ending happiness, the other to everlasting damnation.

After his training and his subsequent ordination in 1817, Ridgeway became pastor of the Hanley Congregational Church in the Potteries district of North Staffordshire. This church was called 'The Tabernacle', a name that he uses again later. Ridgeway was described as a 'fire and brimstone' preacher, a person who evoked a strong personal following because of his concerns about his parishioners. At least one of his sermons, 'The Apostles' Commission', was published and a copy of it is held in the National Library of Australia, in Canberra.

Soon after being ordained in 1817, he married Jane Sophia Benning. The first of his four children, Watts, was born in 1820, with two further sons, Ridgway (note spelling without an 'e') and Simpson and then a daughter, Sophia. Simpson was born in 1822, although this particular Simpson son is a minor part of this book, since he died when thirteen years old, as will be subsequently explained.

Despite his purchase of a thirty-acre farm, Thorny Hedge, about five miles from the town of Hanley, the origin of Ridgeway's interest in agriculture is unclear. While it may have materially assisted the wellbeing of a growing family, the record shows the farm was not a highly productive one. Given his pastoral duties, Ridgeway was a weekend farmer and his boys regularly assisted him when they were old enough. It seems likely that hard work was a necessity if any produce was to be gained from the soil of marginal worth on this property.

In 1825, when Ridgeway was thirty-five years old, his wife died, leaving him with four small children, the youngest of whom, Sophia, also died three years later. Ridgeway remarried thirteen months later. His second wife was Martha Keeling, with whom he had six more children, Martha, Sophia, William, Catherine, Simpson and Sarah. Simpson (the second use of that name) was born in 1835 and it is he who is a key figure in this account, with his five sons constituting the major part of this book. The half-brother, Watts, whose descendants are acknowledged, is not included in this account, nor are Simpson's sisters and their descendants.

Life in the industrial towns of England at that time would now be hard to imagine. Records show that Hanley, a town of about 3000 dwellings, was not particularly attractive and lacked proper sanitation and regular removal of waste. Apart from other industries, twenty-five pottery kilns added their smoke to that produced by the fires in the houses. These conditions were hardly conducive to raising a large family. Notwithstanding these trying circumstances, it appears that Ridgeway was regarded by others as a strong-minded man, confident of his abilities, a man with a firm sense of duty, justice and discipline – characteristics that would have fitted well with Congregational church doctrine at that time. Admission to the denomination appears to have involved application for membership and voting by existing members on whether to accept the applicant, based on an interview seeking information about the applicant's convictions. Under this regime, Ridgeway used his energies and influence to the point where the church building in Hanley had to be enlarged to accommodate the members of his flock.

Perhaps Ridgeway's ideological background and his social circumstances at the time prepared him for what lay ahead: a risky and hazardous journey and a loss of familiar surroundings - notwithstanding its disadvantages - to embark on an enterprise that many would shrink from. The contrast between an established ministry in a familiar location on one side of the world and that in another country on the other side, largely unknown except as containing penal colonies, is inconceivable. South Australia had no convict history, but that also meant that it was in effect a social experiment of free enterprise, a young country making its own way, albeit with guidance from the colonisation commissioners and with some reluctant financial assistance after proclamation from the Imperial Government. It was in this 'experiment' that Ridgeway saw opportunity for himself, his large family and those who were prepared to follow him into the unknown. And this says something about the nature of the man himself and the faith, possibly blind, of those who decided to join him in such an extraordinary venture.

This situation was compounded by several factors, not the least of which was that the Congregational church ideology was at odds with the established Church of England, reflecting the class differences and religious inequality strongly prevailing in England at that time. The Congregationalists, or Independents – Dissenters – as a denomination were not immune from religious persecution, finding themselves subject to various social and financial penalties not applied to the established church and its members, a situation clearly against Ridgeway's personal beliefs as 'an ardent believer in freedom, social justice and religious equality'. He upheld these beliefs unwaveringly throughout his lifetime and they became guiding principles for much of what he did and informed the messages he had for others, including his children, as this book attempts to convey.

In addition, economic circumstances at the time were such that Ridgeway had doubts about his capacity to provide adequate support for a large family residing in North England. On the other side of the world, however, the new colony of South Australia was being established, based on the Wakefield Scheme, which highlighted the virtues of an appropriate balance between land availability at a set price, labour to take up and work that land, and capital funds for developing essential facilities. Government support for the concept was provided through the enactment of the *South Australia Act 1834*. Furthermore, key individuals wanted the new colony to be 'godly', reinforced by religious equality. One of these individuals was George Fife Angas, a member of the South Australian Association, who expected the new colony to:

> in the first instance to provide a place of refuge for pious dissenters of Great Britain who could in their new home discharge their consciences before God in civil and religious liberty without any disabilities.

Even though he had presided over an established ministry for over twenty years, Ridgeway was selected by the Colonial Missionary Society to take a band of would-be colonists to South Australia to establish a settlement. Despite the enormity of the decision, he decided to emigrate with his second wife and family of eight children, the eldest of whom was nineteen and the youngest about twelve months. These children were Watts, Ridgway, Martha, Sophia, William, Catherine, Simpson and Sarah. Under the Wakefield Scheme he purchased a land entitlement of five-hundred-and-sixty acres at one pound per acre, which entitled him to include twenty-eight labourers in his party, who were also entitled to free passage. This party arrived at Holdfast Bay on 10 June 1839 on the *Sir Charles Forbes* after a sea voyage of over five months.

Ridgeway arrived in South Australia bearing letters of introduction from Lord Glenelg, Imperial Secretary of State for the Colonies, which were duly presented to Governor Gawler, who, as we have seen, encouraged Ridgeway to take up his land entitlement in the vicinity of Encounter Bay, south of the new city of Adelaide. While most of the party sailed around the coast from Holdfast Bay, the remainder, under the charge of Ridgeway's eldest son Watts, Simpson's half-brother, went overland with stock, guided by two Aboriginal people. They settled at Yilki (then known as Yeilkey), three kilometres west of the outlet of the Inman River. Ridgeway's diary at the time records:

> Landed at Encounter Bay with my wife and 8 children with servants July 1839 and settled on Yeilkey Farm so called by us in honor of the native name of this district which is Yeilkey but called Encounter Bay by Europeans because an English and French vessel met unexpectedly here being on an exploring expedition.

Simpson's 'Old-time memories', referred to earlier, notes 'blacks lining the beach to the great apprehension of the women and children'. A site was chosen on a rise for the encampment, with a circular clearing made by the men, and tents pitched, along with a bough chapel raised in the name of the Lord. Women and children were to be conveyed from the landing spot on the beach by bullock dray. This vehicle had been lent by the head man of the whale fishery located at the western end of Encounter Bay. Working for him was a man who was thought to be a capable teamster. It proved to be otherwise, as the apparently drunken teamster became lost as darkness fell, also managing to dislodge a wheel of the dray somewhere in the heavily timbered bends of the Inman River. Simpson as a young child has vivid memories of this occasion, best described in his words:

> In later days, with the knowledge of bush life that experience brings, a camp for the night under such circumstances would not have been very serious to any there, but to them, as new arrivals, it was full of horrors. A tribe of savages inspiring the utmost fear and terror was in the immediate proximity. No man of their race except a sodden incapable wretch, sunk in a drunken sleep, was near. Surrounded by the impenetrable darkness of the weird Australian forest, the sad sighing of the wind through the sombre sheoak trees, and the distant boom of the old ocean's waves, it must be admitted there was some cause for apprehension. Later, as night advanced, were added to these the appalling howls of the wild dogs slowly gathering nearer. We know now that these were imaginary terrors, but none the less, they were real indeed to the women and children cowering together, fearing a thousand dangers. This was the scene where the first actual consciousness of life began for me. I remember lying down among the foliage of a fallen sheoak tree, under the lee of which the party had taken shelter from the cold night wind … Such was the first night on Australia's shores for many of the contingent who formed the pioneer settlement at Encounter Bay in the year of grace 1839.

Among these seemingly insuperable difficulties were other tests, which in later times would have been at least amusing, if not hilarious, but at the time were less so. Simpson's 'Old-time memories' contain many stories and some are too good to overlook. They certainly reveal that he, in later life and possibly always, had a sense of humour:

> The first real difficulty was how to transfer the tons of luggage and stores from the beach to the tents. Four bullocks had been brought from Adelaide. The colonial way (introduced from NSW) was to work them in wooden yokes and iron bows as is done now. But this revolted the humane soul of the pastor (was not this the new Eden?) and the fiat went forth that Foxy was to be put in harness in the shaft of the cart and Farmer in traces, tandem fashion. The scene was enlivening. The animals were only half broken to begin with, and under the unwonted proceeding of getting harness on there was much careering and capering over the sylvan landscape, men hanging on to ropes attached to unruly and furious steers. At length the repugnant and protesting Foxy was, despite his struggles, placed between the shafts and Farmer in traces before him. Ungrateful brutes, no sooner was the signal given to proceed given by the kind, considerate master, who wished to substitute soft easy collars for hard, cruel, wooden yokes and iron bows, than with a rebellious, angry swish of the tail and a fractious toss of the horns Foxy plunged cart and all over Farmer, who, not to be outdone, lent his assistance to tilt the vehicle upside down. Then there was a scatter of men, bullocks, harness, timber, and temper, and when the tempest had 'dwindled to a calm' there was one convert and that was the parson. The fragments of the harness were collected and put away. A pole was put in the cart in lieu of the broken shafts, the

> yokes and bows brought out, and, failing to understand gentle measures, the unappreciative steers were condemned to labour in them for the rest of their natural lives.

This and other stories from 'Old-time memories' tell us more of the nature of 'the parson' and his iron determination not only to confront extraordinary difficulties but also to prevail one way or the other. Failure was not part of his lexicon, either spiritually or practically; his dilemma was when these two ideals were in conflict. The collective good and the overall need were the prevailing imperatives and these values were clearly on display to all of his 'flock', but particularly to his family, and were inevitably passed on to his children. Leadership was in Ridgeway's blood and was described by Simpson as eloquent yet forceful and impartial yet persuasive, while not demeaning those he was dealing with. This description accords with the concepts of freedom, social justice and religious equality, noted earlier, that drove Ridgeway in all his endeavours. It is inconceivable that such values did not influence Simpson and his siblings, even if only partially.

Further details of early life in Yeilkey, Encounter Bay, are documented by others elsewhere. Needless to say, the realities of an alien landscape, the relative isolation and the necessity of ensuring basic survival, access to shelter, food and water were obstacles to be surmounted, certainly by Ridgeway as the leader. Living in a large tent for two years would test any family. In addition, the spiritual needs of the small community were intrinsic to the lives of the new settlers. Ridgeway ensured, as only he could, that those spiritual needs were imparted in a way that mirrored his own unyielding convictions of right and wrong. In his 'Old-time memories', Simpson describes Ridgeway's preaching style:

> I well remember how what we called his thunder and lightning sermons used to terrify and even revolt me in my childhood days, and not children alone, for I have seen whole congregations listen spellbound with blanched faces when he painted the eternally enduring anguish of the doomed sinner in that seething abode of endless misery.

In terms of living off the land, the types of agricultural practices that might work for farming in England do not necessarily produce results on the other side of the world. Simpson's memoirs refer to the important task of clearing and cultivating the land, with the first crop of grain being sown within three months of arrival at Yeilkey. The parson took on the onerous position of chief bullock driver, using techniques that Simpson describes (when written by him in 1895) as having 'a ludicrous aspect though there is a pathetic side when one thinks what these utterly inexperienced men, both teamsters and farmers encountered'.

The tedious process of grubbing and burning thick timber was necessary for crop sowing and once the trees had been felled there was no lingering to remove tree roots as the grain had to be sown without delay – for everyone had to be fed. This produced another revealing as well as amusing story about the parson in Simpson's 'Old-time memories':

> Abraham Salt was a prize ploughman, having competed in ploughing matches given by no less a person than His Grace the Duke of Sutherland in England. When put between the handles of a light iron plough of English manufacture behind a team of raw bullocks, under the sole guidance of the rev. and energetic but not proficient puncher, he ventured to expostulate and even

> feebly suggested that there existed roots and other impediments to a successful issue.
>
> 'Fear not', said the parson. 'Stick in the plough, man. I am going straight across the clearing to that tree.'
>
> Salt did what he was told and the too-sanguine driver tried to do what he had promised, but Farmer, Foxy and Co. had their own ideas in the matter. I believe, however, they ultimately did reach that tree but it was by a circuitous route, and with the plough and ploughman in a considerably mangled condition. Both implement and workman were obviously better fitted for the smooth meadow lands of old England than to the rough virgin soil of Australia, full of roots and stumps.

According to his son, 'the parson', not to be beaten, had a strong wooden plough of Tasmanian design made to turn the soil; however, this first crop failed, not because of any issues related to its sowing but through lack of fencing. Simpson somewhat unkindly described his father as a far more efficient parson than farmer. Despite this slightly uncharitable description, a family house was built and larger paddocks were cleared and fenced.

Children often assisted with the myriad jobs needing to be done, which conflicted on occasions with Ridgeway's wife Martha's insistence on schooling and education as high priorities, not only for her immediate family, but also for other members of the party of new settlers. She was also a much-loved mother and stepmother who took her mothering responsibilities very seriously. Her son, Simpson, a key person in this narrative, was described as a sickly child and her attention to his needs and to those of her other children is notable, particularly given how Simpson's later life evolved. Indeed, what he achieved over his ninety years was extraordinary.

This account would be incomplete without commenting on Ridgeway's underlying motivation upon arrival in South Australia, summed up in his statement: 'I preach righteousness and practise agriculture'. This maxim was his primary driving force in his adopted country, which his family and others would surely have appreciated, even if they were not so driven. Paddocks were sown to crops with variable success and stock were raised and grazed for meat and milk production. The 'devout soul of the pastor' ensured the early construction of a bough chapel, replaced in 1846 by a limestone building with a polished red gum desk, and again called The Tabernacle. Simpson described it as a small, nearly square, unpretentious place of worship, facing the ocean. Many hands assisted in its construction, including those of the parson. According to Simpson, one of the happiest days of his life was when Ridgeway preached the Word to his followers. As the district developed and the little community heard of other opportunities elsewhere, many moved away and newcomers arrived. The Tabernacle was regularly full and the parson founded other churches in the region, often remote and a test for any person. To quote Simpson:

> 'Woe is me', said the parson, 'if I preach not the gospel', and he preached it, riding long distances over rough wild bush tracks, across bridgeless rivers, rain or shine, or during the darkest, stormiest, winter nights. The only creatures who probably failed to admire such devotion were the horses he rode, and it was surely hard lines on them.
>
> Yet withal not only a parson. A Magistrate, active in the discharge of the duties of the Office, and a very terror to evildoers. For years the Chairman of the Encounter Bay District Council. The Chairman par excellence of all public meetings,

> eloquent, forceful, impartial, he swayed opinion at his will, and yet wounded no man's self esteem. Often asked to represent the district in Parliament, without hesitation he declined, feeling that his higher calling was of vastly greater importance.

Those long distances and rough bush tracks did not deter Ridgeway from fulfilling what, without reservation, he saw as his selfless duty to God and his fellow man and woman. He was the driving force behind church groups at Bald Hills, Port Elliot, Middleton, Goolwa and Currency Creek, all towns within a thirty-mile radius of Yeilkey.

Photo taken in 1947 of where the Tabernacle was built at Encounter Bay, with Constance Mary Newland, the author's mother.

At that time Bald Hills, Currency Creek and Milang were then isolated settlements, Milang being about fifteen miles northeast of Currency Creek. Hindmarsh Island is reported as yet another location at which Ridgeway conducted preaching. Distances such as these mean little in these days of modern roads. Once these places of worship had been established, they had to be serviced regularly, which meant travelling on horseback or by horse and cart, and included crossing flooded creeks. Sometimes Ridgeway would arrive in wet clothes at these locations to fulfil his God-driven obligation to his congregation. He is reported more than once to have walked from Encounter Bay to Adelaide for meetings important to him, not deterred by flooded watercourses over the fifty-five-mile distance. Having walked there, Ridgeway then had to find a way back by whatever means.

After a lifetime of toil and devotion, Ridgeway suffered an untimely and violent death as the result of an accident to the mailcart in which he was travelling on the morning of 8 March 1864 in the hills above Port Elliot. He was seated in the front with the driver, when the pole of the two-wheeled cart broke and Ridgeway and the driver were thrown violently to the ground. They were trampled by the horses, with Ridgeway receiving fatal injuries, including a broken spine. He was dead a few hours later, without seeing his wife and family. He surely would have preferred a different manner of dying, but this was not to be for a 'true soldier of the Christian Cross, dying in harness in the path of duty, steadfast to the last'. An even more violent death occurred over fifty years later to a grandson whom Ridgeway never met.

A tribute in the *South Australian Weekly Chronicle* of 12 March 1864 states:

> With an energy that never tired, with physical endurance far beyond men of much greater stature, and with steadfastness of purpose never exceeded, he was foremost in every cause calculated to promote the interest and welfare of the district in

> which he lived and his fellow colonists in general ... it was he who gave character and tone to any gathering affecting the well-being of the district.

Although such a role model – as both a leader and a father – would have been hard to emulate, undoubtedly some of these characteristics would have been passed on to succeeding generations. The last words of this chapter belong to Newland's son Simpson, the subject of the next chapter, who writes about his father:

> These old Puritans were grand characters and England would be shorn of half its glory if such stern pullers down of kings and dignities [*sic*] had never existed, though their distinctive characteristics excite more admiration than affection.

Simpson at the time of his father's untimely death was living at Marra in New South Wales. He had just taken stock to Adelaide, several hundred miles away, on horseback, largely across country, and had returned to Marra when he received news of his father's accidental death by mail. Undaunted, he saddled his horse and rode back those hundreds of miles to South Australia – as a son of Ridgeway would do as a matter of course. That in itself is devotion and a great sense of duty.

3

Paving the way

A 'sickly' four-year-old boy called Simpson accompanied his parents, Ridgeway and Martha Newland, and his several siblings from England on the six-month voyage to South Australia on the 400-ton sailing ship, the *Sir Charles Forbes*, arriving at Holdfast Bay on 7 June 1839. This child, who grew to a man of small stature (around 5 feet or 152.5 cm), not only survived such a voyage, but also went on to achieve a great deal over his life of about ninety years, along the way championing many causes. The same sickly boy became a man who was daunted by very little, often displaying courage bordering on the foolhardy as he confronted his various challenges. And to compound his often extreme lifestyle, during his life he endured periods of extraordinary loneliness and isolation. A relatively quietly spoken person, he achieved milestones that some might dream about and others may find barely believable. He was clearly regarded as something of a prodigy by his parents, both of whom he clearly respected, although the direction of his life was markedly different from theirs.

In some ways, his character is largely unsurprising. While he certainly held strong convictions about decency, honesty and the importance of making his mark in a growing colonial community – as did his father Ridgeway – he did not go into the ministry. Simpson travelled extensively in an increasingly settled Australia and saw and experienced much about which his parents had little or no knowledge. That is not to suggest that what he did was less commendable than the extraordinary achievements of his parents: inevitably, the context and circumstances were different. His father was driven to minister to what he saw as the godly needs of others finding their respective ways in an isolated and growing community. In doing so, Ridgeway showed remarkable patience, thoughtfulness, courage and sheer determination under conditions hard to imagine now nearly two hundred years later.

Yet even a cursory examination of Simpson's life shows the Ridgeway characteristics alive and well in his son and which, along with others, made up Simpson's complex personality. With the benefit of hindsight, it appears almost as if Simpson chose to make the first half of his life the ultimate test of human endurance, given the privations and ever-present danger to life and limb that characterised the path to his accomplishments. While Simpson's very significant later achievements in public life are known to some, his private and understated nature has meant that many of his earlier activities have not been publicly known until now. He was not an arrogant man and it is not surprising that relatively little detailed information about his life is available.

As far as I am aware, the photograph of Simpson in his mid-thirties on page 43 has not been published before. It shows a man of great determination: a strong face and imposing beard possibly made up for his diminutive stature and gives a different impression from the later 'statesman' photograph that is normally used.

Fortunately, many of his letters and associated documentation have been retained by his descendants. Much of what is contained in this book is based on this evidence, which reveals an extraordinary life, one lived in remarkable circumstances, the details of which are largely unknown, including by some of his descendants. It is impossible to identify a contemporary person who might be Simpson's equivalent since the circumstances of a twenty-first century existence are so unlike those he experienced in the mid- and late nineteenth century.

Simpson married later in life than most, at thirty-eight years. His new wife Jane Isabella Layton, a school teacher, was twenty-one years old. She bore five sons, around whom this narrative revolves. The sons' stories are equally engaging, as will be revealed, particularly two of the older sons, who were fortunate to live long lives.

As with their father and his father, these five sons were 'men' in the traditional sense, not surprising, given their circumstances and the filial expectations across generations, both spoken and unspoken. Simpson, when growing up, was regularly exposed to his father Ridgeway's unswerving views on righteousness, which probably did him little harm. Notwithstanding Ridgeway's religious convictions, Simpson appears not to have thrust such views down the throats of his sons. He did however want them to know the difference between right and wrong, as had his father before him. Simpson clearly wanted to make his mark, but in his own way and under his terms. He sought opportunities that inevitably involved hard work and exposed him to the significant risks that presented themselves in a relatively unexplored young country, where, with effort, an individual might make a fortune. In many ways, largely through his own efforts, he was successful in achieving this.

It is possible that his early life and the drive of his parents materially assisted Simpson to achieve what he did. While they could well have helped him financially, their contribution was more about establishing foundations on which he could build his own life and fortune, as distinct from the benefits of any significant inherited wealth. He had what it took to see opportunities and he grasped them, irrespective of the potential difficulties, and this is the enduring characteristic he appeared to gain from his parents. It is interesting to speculate on why Simpson achieved so much, and yet his own siblings appear not to have had such an obvious drive and indomitable spirit for undertaking on such challenges. Simpson was a successful squatter, politician, author and, for many, a statesman. Whether he was a successful parent is for others to decide. It seems that from what is known about his children that they were grateful for his wisdom, occasional generosity and their heritage.

Simpson Newland, CMG, was born on 2 November 1835 at Hanley, the Potteries in Staffordshire, England. His achievements as a prominent South Australian flowed from the resolve of his parents, both of whom were a guiding influence and inspiration for him. His mother Martha was highly educated, gifted in classical studies and proficient in Hebrew, Latin and French. She was also a natural teacher. She was instrumental in educating Simpson and his seven sisters and brothers under conditions that would challenge the most resolute of teachers. It is notable that Simpson himself also married a schoolteacher.

His father Ridgeway, as already described, was of Puritan background with an iron will, whose single aim in life was devotion to duty. He saw the newly formed colony of South Australia as an opportunity to be free from the many disadvantages which religious non-conformists suffered in England. He had a vision of an ideal settlement and the chance to prosper through personal endeavour. Interestingly, Ridgeway's grandson Victor Marra, whose story is also described below, had a not dissimilar vision when he went to British East Africa as a new settler after the Boer War over seventy years later.

As a boy Simpson would have experienced the joy and wonder of the strange coastal environment at Encounter Bay, where Ridgeway and his party settled after their arrival, as well as the privations and sheer difficulty of literally establishing a place to survive and prosper in the unfamiliar South Australian bush. The responsibility assumed by his parents, not only for themselves and their children, but also for others in the fledging community, must have been the ultimate test in faith and perseverance. His father's determination to 'preach righteousness and practise agriculture' and to make a success of the new and growing community at Encounter Bay must have had considerable influence on his children generally and clearly on Simpson.

Newspaper articles written about Simpson upon his death in June 1925 give some insight into his situation as a young boy. Encounter Bay in the 1830s and for the years following was a location for whale hunting, with Rosetta Head, or the Bluff, as it has been known for many years, being the observation point to detect whales for hunting and harvesting. The whalers themselves were hardy men who had adopted an unenviable way of earning a living, given the dangers and sheer discomfort of hunting creatures such as Southern Right Whales from an open boat, where the crew's strength, manpower and ingenuity, combined with teamwork, determined their survival. The extracts from the newspapers assert that it was among such whaling men that Simpson saw and experienced a way of life, both romantic and fraught with risk, that was not necessarily to his parents' liking. From such men, as well as from the local

Indigenous people of the Narrinyeri (now Ngarrindjeri) tribe, Simpson started to build a store of knowledge about early settlement conditions for both the white settlers and local indigenous people.

Although Simpson wrote his highly informative – and useful to this narrative – memoirs late in his life, *Memoirs of Simpson Newland CMG*, the information contained in them about his early life is provided in general terms only. Clearly his parents were a major influence and he is unequivocal about them:

> The examples of parents to children is most important. On all natures it must have some effect, while on many, it exercises lasting influence. In this respect I was particularly fortunate, for there never was a son blessed with better parents. My father was a grand old man, who lived his life as few have lived. At all times upright and honourable, he could straighten out the difficulties and lighten the burdens of all who sought his aid. Often the work seemed hard, particularly at harvest time, yet we all realised that he did his best to render it light. By undertaking as much as possible of the difficult portions himself, he would inspire those about him with energy and courage. Merely to think of him in the years that followed never failed to produce sentiments of lively appreciation and keen admiration.

In addition, in his 'Old-time memories' of 1895, Simpson does not so much refer to himself but to his parents and the conditions under which they lived at Yeilkey, making the best of their circumstances, as already described. In his *Memoirs* Simpson refers to his mother Martha in eloquent and tender terms as a person who had a great influence on him. Perhaps his late marriage to a school teacher was influenced, at least in part, by her:

> In all these things she [his mother] who as a woman, wife, and mother occupied the first place, set no limits to her endeavours to benefit all, particularly the young. She early formed a night school, and thus assiduously taught the youth that must otherwise have grown up in ignorance. Looking back through the long years it is the subject for marvel what that frail, gently nurtured lady accomplished under a condition of things so adverse. The younger members of her own family to educate, for her they certainly owed all they ever learned, beside the thousand and one responsibilities of a large household. A classical Hebrew scholar, and unquestionably the deepest read of all the men and women I have met, she was more than qualified for all of this. Think of the difficulties, the bitter trials, the wearing anxieties of the wild bush life, the total absence of luxuries but of many of what we now consider absolute necessaries of existence, and then realise if you can what all this meant to such a one and thank God that a few women 'only a little lower than the angels' now and then live to show us what human nature at its best is capable of. Few are left of those she so patiently, earnestly taught, but if any read these lines their heart will throb in response to the remembrance of the gentle loving soul to whom they are so indebted.

While this beautifully written tribute says much about Martha, it also says something about Simpson and the extent of his publicly professed love and admiration for his mother and his gratitude for what she gave to him, including her role on moulding his character and personality.

Simpson's stepbrothers Watts and Ridgway were an important part of his education about farming and grazing. The elder stepbrother Ridgway in effect took charge of his father's sheep, which required shepherding, as there were no fences. Simpson learnt things from these stepbrothers both as a boy and young man that served him well in later life. Since his *Memoirs* reveal much about him, I have quoted extensively from this work to emphasise what he was like and what he became:

> My stepbrother Ridgway, eleven years older than I, and strong and healthy, was thought a great deal of by the whole settlement, and my father particularly looked upon him as a young man of great promise. Naturally, I envied him, but at the same time I considered him to be rather conceited, and used to tell him I would beat him in the long run. Evidently, therefore, I had some latent ambition in those early days, and as time went on, and I grew stronger, I became my brother's rival in many ways. I was early taught to plough and sow, and reap, drive bullock teams, shear sheep, handle stock, and ride horses … Milking cows and driving them to and from pasture had its compensations, but best of all was the fun of riding calves full speed around the stacks. Minding sheep, with my head buried in a book, or talking to the whalers was not without interest.

Simpson recounts that 'fascinating excursions along the beach, searching for shells and other objects of interest' were regular childhood activities. One of his favourite spots in the Encounter Bay locality was the Bluff itself, best illustrated in his own words, indicating that its romance and beauty were clearly imprinted on his personality:

> I write of the grand old Bluff as I first remember it. It was the first feature of importance in Encounter Bay. It stood out paramount in the whole beautiful scene – the perfect land and water scape. The coastline was an unforgettable spectacle of rugged grandeur and

> soft beauty, first closing in that marvel of loveliness, Petrel Bay, and then stretching away westward to Waitpinga, Cape Jervis and beyond. Within these lay a sweep of glorious headlands, fringed by white spray leaping from the vast Southern Ocean as it fell on those lonely shores.

The books and stories written by Simpson during his life and his choice of words and language show a strong sense of romance, in combination with eloquent expression. We can only surmise that these early memories must have exerted a great impact on his perceptions of the world around him. He retained his connection with the Encounter Bay landscape for most of his life, including having a house at Victor Harbor in his later years, not far from where he came ashore with his family in 1839. His five sons were welcome there too and often visited. Simpson's knowledge of the locality must have been extensive, as he tended his father's flocks of sheep and herd of cattle for several years before renting the family property himself, which, when originally taken up by his father, consisted of over 500 acres. *Memoirs* makes clear that Simpson's ambition was to open up new country and venture out on his own. Renting his father's farm was a means for him to learn the further skills necessary to do so. Hard work during the day on the farm willingly done, and hard study at night willingly under his mother's guidance took him through his teenage years and beyond.

From other information obtained from *Memoirs*, we know that Simpson's father grazed cattle over a wide area of the south coast beyond the 500 acres, from the Waitpinga river west to Cape Jervis. This country is dotted with many hills and gullies, and Simpson and his brother Ridgway were often out on horseback for a week at a time, tending to these cattle. In Simpson's own words:

> I had a splendid horse called 'Ivanhoe', which was one of the best I have ever owned, and on this fine animal I did a great deal of hard riding over rough country, rounding up wild cattle. A ready sale was always to be found for animals in good condition in Willunga and the surrounding district, and the delivery of them was an undertaking fraught with many difficulties and dangers, but the experience I gained in those early years fitted me for the still more arduous bush life that was before me. Some of those wild, dangerous rides were intensely exciting, and even now, in far-off retrospect, the memory of them warms my blood.
>
> Being so constantly in the saddle, I became a very good horseman.

These are prophetic words, as the remainder of this chapter will reveal.

As with other events in Simpson's remarkable life, the 'very good horseman' comment is something of an understatement, if family evidence of his activities is anything to go by. Much of his life was inextricably linked with horses, to the extent he may well have spent more time with various horses during his life than with some people! His attachment to horses is revealed several times in his books and this is not surprising, considering the enormous amount of time Simpson spent in the saddle, the horse being the principal form of transport. Also for him on occasions horsemanship represented success or failure and sometimes life or death. Physically, he must have been the ideal rider, being, according to his letters, very light (around 9 stone 2 pounds or 59 kg in middle age). The Mt McPherson wild mob story recounted later in this chapter is one of many examples of his skill and daring with horses, an episode that could have ended badly, had he been anything but a small, yet plucky, man. In their father, his sons undoubtedly had a highly experienced teacher and role model. All became good horsemen, and some relations in my generation have maintained this skill.

Prior to his twenty-first birthday, according to his *Memoirs*, Simpson travelled with his brother-in-law-to-be, Henry Field, by sea to Sydney, where they bought cattle from Goulburn, subsequently driving them overland to Adelaide. This was the first time such a venture had been undertaken over a distance of several hundred miles of largely trackless country, and the lessons that Simpson had earlier learnt from his half-brother Ridgway and others must have contributed to the success of this venture. It is understood that he had a similar experience with sheep from the Adelaide region and, acting as a drover himself, brought them safely to Wentworth in New South Wales, where they were to form the basis of flocks on various stations on the Darling River, including his own properties. Such undertakings are today hard to imagine, and Simpson's skill in bushcraft, along with his increasing interest in the Aborigines of the areas through which he passed, must have stood him in good stead. The characteristics of planning, self-reliance, courage and capacity for sheer hard work were becoming increasingly evident in Simpson, including an understanding of animals and horsemanship. He also was a keen observer of what was around him, which seemed to initiate a yearning to record his observations and eventually commit them to paper. In his words:

> Perhaps during these first years of isolation came my earliest desires to write my thoughts. To my mind the man is dull indeed, who, after spending years in the wilds, is not impressed by the beauties and wonders of Nature. In my loneliness my thoughts and musings provided interesting company, and perhaps proved

the incentive to the writings of later days, most of which are descriptive of Australian life. Solitude taught me to think, and the bush became an absorbing theme.

Simpson Newland c. 1865.

While Simpson's exact age when he actively entered the pastoral industry is not known, the evidence points to its being when he was in his late twenties or early thirties. He was offered and accepted a financial interest in Marra and Warlo stations on the Darling River in New South Wales and later Talyealye station on the Paroo River near the Queensland border. He was initially in partnership with his brother-in-law-to-be, Henry Field of South Australia, and Charles and Andrew Chisolm of New South

Wales. This time, up to his marriage in 1872, must have been one of unbelievable loneliness, punctuated by wild adventure. He undertook the seven-hundred-mile trip from Adelaide to Warlo and Marra on his own through country unknown to him, guided only by the Murray and Darling rivers. Not only did he have to cope with the unknown, he was confronted by floodwaters over a wide area, which would have made navigating his way more difficult along and through those flooded waterways. On occasions he was fortunate, in that he finished the last part of this journey by river steamer.

His arrival at Marra and his fifteen or so years residing there allowed him to gain an on-ground knowledge of what we now know as the Murray–Darling Basin. Simpson's *Memoirs* refer to immense possibilities waiting to be tapped and he saw a role for himself in its development, as will be seen.

During Simpson's time on the Darling, he was tested in so many ways. He had to deal with wild cattle, as well as floodwaters up to ten miles wide, initially with no boat or other way round such floods. He became a strong and courageous swimmer and competent boatman. He regularly interacted with the Aboriginal people living traditional lives, and they clearly resented the arrival of Europeans with sheep and cattle, which changed the nature of the land of their birthright. He worked closely with some, recognising their skill and their close association with the landscape.

He had to manage and deal with European itinerant stockman and other workers, some of whom clearly had dubious backgrounds. Droving cattle from Marra to Adelaide took eight weeks on horseback through country largely unoccupied by Europeans, necessarily demanding a high degree of self-reliance, skill, sheer toughness and tenacity. As explained earlier, Simpson heard of the accident and death of his father in early 1864 by mail delivered to Marra soon after he had returned on horseback from one of these long trips. Another journey of such length would daunt most, but as a devoted son he retraced his route of around seven hundred miles to be with his family to honour his late father's memory.

The existence on Marra of the Undelcarra rocks is likely to have made him contemplate the deep meaning of landscape and its natural features to Aboriginal people. Having seen the Undelcarra rocks on part of the original Marra (now on a separate pastoral property known as Polocara), I can testify to the indefinable presence of something unusual if not mystical in this locality. This situation must have resonated with Simpson, given the later adoption of the Undelcarra name for his Adelaide house in the foothills suburb of Burnside.

Undelcarra Rocks in 2012, now on Polocara.

In the mid-1860s and through the 1870s, Simpson, with assistance from his cousin James Wark, managed a large pastoral enterprise comprised of around 80,000 sheep and 15,000 cattle. He worked to improve the quality of the stock to make the most of the enterprise, employing both Aboriginal and European shepherds; he was forced to take action when one of the latter began to wield a knife, threatening both him and other men. Yet Simpson was not only a squatter; he was also a close observer of nature around him and he had an abiding interest in the plants, birds and animals of the country, about which he wrote in *Memoirs*. He also described in detail the region's Aboriginal people, their customs and their interaction with the whiteman or 'Boree'. He referred to particular personalities, including Barpoo, the recognised leader of the local Aborigines, whom he described as:

> tall, spare, stately; in manner quiet, reserved, and dignified, so far as any white man could judge, for he never unbent to them. Indeed from first to last he refused to hold any intercourse with the hated Boree, much less work for him, wear his clothes, or even eat his food.

Simpson clearly admired this man greatly for his stand against the mounting tide of European settlement and goes on to say in *Memoirs*:

> When Barpoo was hungry, he doubtless killed a sheep or robbed a hut of rations, and, as already intimated, I have little doubt that he knocked lonely travellers on the head as opportunity offered. But have not many of the heroic patriots of history done all these things against the enemies and despoilers of their country? Cool reflection suggests something of what that fierce, untameable spirit must have felt when he saw the detested interloper take

> possession of all his country, after slaughtering many of his people in their vain attempts at resistance, making shepherds and stockmen of the free hunters, then later to see them wither and die. There was clearly nothing left for him but to die cursing the Boree.

Such words and opinions would not have endeared him to some of his European associates. Given that Simpson himself was one of the 'cursed Boree', his observations on and attitude towards the Aboriginal people he came to know showed respect, and he admired their capacity to live in and use the environment around them. At the same time, in spite of himself, he seemed to show superiority over them. Terms such as 'faithful slave' do not appear often and he refers to one 'black' (a term commonly used, which inevitably must be demeaning) as 'one of the truest gentlemen I have ever seen'. This is generous and genuine praise. Given the time of his writings, he showed a considerably enlightened view not replicated and probably not supported by many of his peers. After all, history shows that shootings and massacres of Aborigines were still occurring around the time that Simpson was at Marra, even if not widely known and reported at the time.

Other tests for this remarkable man came in the form of bushrangers. He was also called upon to resolve violent disputes between wives and disenchanted husbands, which involved his being threatened by a tomahawk. His prowess as a horseman was well known locally and he could hold his own against anyone, European or Aboriginal. He converted one of the many extraordinary events in which he was intimately involved into a short story. This astonishing incident, involving wild cattle residing in the Mt McPherson Range north of Marra, has been unknown until now and was written in longhand by Simpson early in the twentieth century. His courage and persistence are clearly on display – combined with a degree of what some would see as foolhardiness. It is reproduced in full below, as it exhibits so much of the nature and mettle of a man who would not be beaten by odds that many would regard as overwhelming, if not impossible. It begs the question of what else may have happened at Marra about which he did not write – there may be many such stories.

How we 'broke up' the Mt McPherson Wild Mob

By Simpson Newland, author of *Paving the Way* etc.

(Undated, probably written between 1900 and 1910)

Don't let this title deceive you, there is, in fact, nothing about bushrangers. It's only a yarn about wild cattle and hard riding with quite spice enough of danger to render it exciting.

It was quite in the early days, a few years after the Upper Darling was first stocked. I was then only recently promoted to be the head working Boss in the actual management of the station & burning to prove myself competent to fill the position & worthy of the confidence placed in me. There was a big area of country about a thousand square miles almost equally divided into two runs, one partially stocked with cattle, the other with sheep.

The duties of the manager were certainly not light. Barely sufficient hands were employed to do the necessary work & he was expected to have a close eye on the minutest particular, not merely to supervise but to take the most active & prominent part in everything, from lambing down a flock of ewes to mustering the herd of cattle, whether it were for fats for market or calves to brand. When everyone else on the station could reasonably suppose his work for the day over, the Boss not infrequently had a long ride before him, preparatory to beginning again at daylight, on the opposite side of the run. Or it might be the less congenial task of posting up the monthly accounts & writing letters for the mail. There was no doubt about the hardness of the life but somehow it brought out all the metal there was in a man and forged more. Rarely was a bed slept in, indeed to such an extent was disregard or contempt of indulgence carried, that a blanket often formed no part of the equipment, a saddle cloth forming the only cloak in which the hardy bushman wrapped himself when he sought his repose. Saturated with sweat from the reeking steed it formed but a sorry couch, even after the occupier had in a fastidious moment, dined at the camp fire before seeking rest. Stockyards were few in those days & there were many nights during which long watches had to be kept round restless herds. On such occasions, the Boss must take the hardest & longest, liable also when his watch was over to be called at any moment should occasion arise, as was often the case. A sudden start of the restive brutes impatient to be gone, the approach of scrubbers or a wild bull & in obedience to orders the chief was roused. Foremost in toil, danger or difficulty the Boss occupied the first position & if equal to the post men soon learned to depend on him & look up to him with a deep respect. But he must never show the white feather or in any way prove himself a weakling or gone for ever was his influence over such spirits. Whoever blenched in the drafting yard among the wild cattle when 'rushers' ran 'amuck' he must stand firm or if momentarily compelled to step up the fence it must be in the coolest manner & never over it. What was laughed at & forgiven in a subordinate was cowardice & a disgrace in the chief. White man or black pardoned no faltering in the man who aspired to lead them. If a river or raging torrent had to be crossed the chief must be the first to force his steed over. Or in the mad gallop down the steep stony declivity, thro' the thick interlaced timber or over the breakneck honeycombed ground, the master ever led the way.

Mt McPherson is the south east termination of the range of that name. It is covered with great rocks & loose stones on all the loftier parts, among which bushes of various kinds manage to subsist. The more accessible portions are, or rather were, densely wooded before the combined efforts of cattle, sheep, fire, the axe of man & rabbits, the most effective of all – thinned them. Mulga predominated generally growing in thick masses around the great hill in bush form with boughs interlaced but on the more level land after attaining considerable height with straight stems. A country in which a novice was lost at once for there is nothing to guide him in the close monotonous growth & even the experienced bushman might easily 'get slewed' if the sun became clouded over. Just the very country wild animals retreat to in their efforts to escape from their great persecutor – man.

The Mount McPherson wild mob was made up of a collection of untameable brutes from all the country around. A number were old raker bullocks escaped from a herd of store cattle travelling to Queensland from Williams' Gol Gol station on the Murray, born and bred mallee scrubbers, as hard & wild as bad blood & breeding & rough country could make them. Great long legged horny brutes, mostly browns, blacks or brindles, with huge heavy horns polished to brightness on the outsides by contact with the timber in forcing their way through. There were a proportion of cows fully as fierce & possibly uglier still, occasionally one of these heavy in calf or with a young calf at foot was caught out in the open & yarded, in all probability to be promptly shot.

Among the latter were a considerable proportion of misshapen, barren or speyed females that never bred & they were the worst of an irreclaimable lot. Add to these some cleanskin young stock & bulls that had never seen a yard, a few of the latter hoary with age & the embodiment of ferocity & it must be acknowledged they were as awkward a lot to wheel out of mulga so thick you could scarcely see your hand before you as could be found in broad Australia. They knew every yard of the rocky mountain glades &, to horsemen, the all but impervious masses of close interlocked timber. Beneath lower boughs they threaded their way at a gallop under the eyes of the baffled horseman. I vow I have often only been able to tell which way they were going by the quivering of the foliage of the bushes above caused by their striking against the stems below in their flight. Of course this was when the growth was sufficiently dwarfed to see over from the elevation of the saddle. Again & again have I camped near their feeding ground & at earliest dawn tracked them up in the vain hope of catching them in the fairly open country. Useless trouble, the wary brutes would be in, or close to the edge of their fastnesses, then there was a hurried glimpse of colour, the sound of rushing feet & crashing timber. A short furious gallop thro' stiff spiked mulga in which the rider's life was set upon a die from which the boldest might shrink & they were gone. True by splendid daring an accomplished bush rider mounted on a grand stock horse of the true old breed, might head them but they melted away in the scrub as if they had sank into the earth. The mere effort by horse & man of forcing their way thro' that all but impenetrable tangle wore them down & when they emerged torn & bloody it was well if the steed at least was not lamed for weeks. Almost before thinking of his own wounds it was fortunate indeed if the rider had not to extract with infinite difficulty from between hoof & hair & may be elsewhere one or more stiff sharp mulga spikes so poisonous that to leave them in for a short time was often to lame a valuable horse for life.

But there were other experiences with this mob. Possibly they were surprised in a locality more favourable to the horseman. I will relate one of many such instances. It was one bright spring morning when there was a heavy dew on the grass making tracking easy. A stockman blackboy & myself had dropped across the trail soon after daylight & following it hard overtook the scrubbers in a narrow glade running up the mountain. Hearing us they were off in a moment at a gallop. I was mounted on a fine old stock horse called Billy Button, perhaps the best, taking him all round, of the many good ones it has been my joy to ride & certainly the roughest. He was a long low bay with black points & not a white hair on him. Fast for his build, legs of iron & wonderful muscle which perhaps accounted for his extraordinary roughness. As for his pluck no horse ever foaled was truer grit. On the fairly open country there were his superiors for pace and quality but in rough parts & timber Billy Button was unrivalled if his rider had the courage to let him go & guide him. Nor was much of that necessary the old hero knew his work so well. He seemed to extend himself until he lay almost along the ground & so he passed under the overhanging boughs. His rider frequently had to stretch along one side or the other to escape being torn off & yet often received unavoidable blows. Going at Billy's fastest pace that was inevitable.

Up the glade a beaten cattle track led along this, the wily brutes persistently ran refusing to turn off either to the right or left knowing well that they would thus lose the advantage of the beaten path. Giving the old horse his head I several times, where the ground looked more promising, tried to head them but what with rocks & timber it was impossible & cut them off from the mountain I could not. Presently we rose the spur of the hill where there were fewer stones & the mulga was more stunted. Now was the time. Billy Button seemed to know it & with a grand effort he tore through the bushes to the right of the mob & swung them away from the mountain. On, in a cloud of dust, levelling trees in their mad rush the herd careered down the declivity in the desired direction. I knew there was a little plain of soft red sand honeycombed by native rats, in front. It was only a few acres, surrounded by thick straight stemmed mulga, but large enough to check the mob on, if I could head them before they reached the timber on the further side, & my assistants arrived in time to meet them when they turned. Splendid animal as Billy was in rotten ground he now laboured heavily but I put him at his utmost speed thro' the barbed mulga spars on to & across the loose sand flat taking a dry creek in a flying stride & at the very verge of the far side of the plain turned them round. It appeared the moment of victory & triumph but proved that of defeat. My fine old horse suddenly sank to his knees in the treacherous sand and turned a complete somersault. In the fall my foot got locked in the stirrup & could not get free & had Billy Button not been able to rise quickly it might have fared badly with me. But utterly exhausted by the gallop & fall this was impossible. At last we rose together, I clambering on him on the off side, my leg still jammed in the iron. The scrubbers were gone, however, beyond the hope of recovery & so that had to be added to the many abortive attempts to capture them. Poor old Billy was seriously lamed for some time by mulga stakes, one forced deeply between hoof and hair of his off fore foot I recollect we had great difficulty in extracting. As for myself my riding boots were pierced in several places & clothes torn to tatters not to particularise personal lacerations and contusions.

I had long ere this determined that the wild mob must be broken up, & my defeat whetted that resolve. They were growing in number & doing immense harm to the herd by unsettling them. I thought of shooting the brutes in their haunts but that was no easy task in thick timber & to get them out seemed well nigh impossible. In fact I did attempt it with small success. To carry a loaded rifle at full speed in such country to get within shot was no pleasant matter & a revolver was not effective. Then among the mob were many beasts much too valuable to be shot down & wasted. A friend at this juncture begged to be allowed to try. He was a great sportsman, a much better shooter than rider. But one attempt was sufficient. He never saw more than the first gleam of a flying scrubber & never afterwards wanted to leave his jumbucks. Soon after this the waters in the back country failed in consequence of summer being well advanced & a long continuance of dry weather. I had been after the brutes on & off for over a fortnight while mustering fat cattle for market. These were now ready to start & I was much annoyed & disappointed that the cream of the wild mob was not among them. There was one more chance. The moon was about at the full & I determined to watch for them at one of the few waterholes remaining. It was situated in a billabong running thro' a rotten plain which flooded whenever there was a 'banker' in the river. There were many objections to this plan. Their coming to this particular hole was very uncertain as tho' it was the furthest out & so nearest to their haunts, there were several other waters in the same creek to which they might resort on that particular night. Then again the ground was dreadfully rotten & cracked, great fissures opening out in all directions, at all times dangerous to gallop over at night. It was little less than suicidal & under the most favourable circumstances with such a quarry much galloping was inevitable. Away from the influence of floods the country was firm but as it rose above the level of the plain it became covered with dead mulga. Years before a fire had swept along the rising ground in a strip killing but not burning the timber. Thousands of the trunks still stood like spectres of the past, a grey white colour with the limbs stretching out like arms. These were bad enough to race through in the imperfect light with the compensation that the smaller boughs were brittle & broke easily but heaven help you if you met a strong one or struck a trunk. Immediately beyond these where the fire had not penetrated grew the forest thick enough to daunt most riders in broad daylight. At night the very instant a mob of scrubbers entered its fringe they were safe from the finest rider & the best horse that ever swept over Australian pastures.

Altogether the distance across the plain over the open & thro' the dead timber to the forest was about three miles. Certainly the surroundings were not favourable for such an undertaking but there was the chance of hearing them coming in the distance & being prepared to surround them at the water, without giving them an opportunity to make a rush for it. It seemed inconceivable that fifty head of cattle could approach without making a sound that sharp ears could distinguish, yet this is precisely what occurred.

Choosing a night near the full moon, I rode, accompanied by a stockman and a blackboy named Jack, as evening fell, to the waterhole already mentioned. The whiteman was one of the party of drovers who were about to start with the mob of fat cattle to market & not one of the station employees. Selected as being a good rider & accustomed to night work, Jack was keen eyed as a hawk, a magnificent tracker tho' that quality could be of no use on such an occasion. A good bold horseman picked because he knew more about the habits of the wild mob than any of his countrymen. That being acknowledged he was considered entitled to participate in an uncommon & honourable service. He also possessed the additional qualification for such an exploit of absolute silence unless imperative necessity compelled him to speak. It must be admitted that he occasionally laughed but if amused himself, decidedly he did not impart any amusement to others. Nay he was so obstinately dumb as to be not only a dull but often a most exasperating companion. Necessary information had to be dragged from him in reluctant monosyllables until the interrogator's patience gave way to strong language. Nor was this all: each movement & action was characterised by the same silence. There was therefore not the slightest possibility that Jack would alarm the approaching scrubbers by any noise whatever.

Three of the best stockhorses were chosen, the redoubtable Billy Button being my mount. He was in splendid fettle (as indeed they all were) fit to jump out of his skin & if a long gallop was inevitable I felt confident of his pluck & condition to go thro' it splendidly. Of course that was not anticipated as we hoped to effect the capture by surprise tho' where such subtle brutes were concerned it was impossible to conjecture what desperate break they might make even when rounded up.

As the sun went down we arrived at the waterhole now reduced to half its dimensions by the long continued dry weather tho' still about two hundred yards in length. Surrounded by a clump of box trees sufficiently close together to form ample cover for our horses from the prying eyes of the wild cattle as they drew near. As the pad along which they were expected to come in led to the lower end of the waterhole which was nearly devoid of timber, we made our camp at the upper end. That is we hitched the horses by the reins to the trees, saddles on their backs ready to be mounted at a moment's warning. Of course there could be no fire or such luxuries as blankets allowed. The former undoubtedly would be seen or smelt by the wary quarry & the latter might conduce to a sleep too sound for the alertness demanded by such an enterprise. The night was divided into three watches, one of the party being on guard at a time, the others lying down to get what rest they could on mother earth's bare bosom. Total silence was strictly enjoined, the man on watch having instructions to nip incipient snoring at the earliest sputter. We anticipated that the cattle would come about midnight & as I was anxious to be up then, Jack was given the first watch with orders to call me in a couple of hours. I believe I dozed part of the brief time allowed by the sable youth but certainly fell into no sound sleep. He intimated in the briefest whisper that nothing of the 'bullockoo' herd had approached, with the conscientious accuracy of a true bushman to 'do his time' but not one minute of the next man's. Jack had roused me almost to the second & promptly proceeded to stretch his form on its natural couch. I crept away & seated myself in the shadow at the trunk of a tree, giving a full view of the plain across which the scrubbers must come. Hour followed hour, owls hooted in the grove, waterfowl splashed in the pool, curlews shrieked shrilly on the plain around & wild dogs howled dismally in the recesses of the forest but there was no sign or sound of the animals we watched for. Midnight came & passed & for a while the small fry sank into a silence that had a more creepy feeling even than listening to the dingos or curlews' mournful wails. The sky became overcast & I could no longer see many paces beyond the timber much less distinguish any object on the plain. All the more necessity to listen attentively. So possessing my soul in patience I waited until it appeared hopeless to linger longer. The thirsty brutes must have gone into water lower down, I thought, or could they have seen, heard, or suspected anything & so escaped us. They could not have smelt us for what light air there was blew steadily from the mountain.

It was now far too dark to see them approach if they did come & as I must trust entirely to my ears I thought I might as well be at the camp. Besides it was prudent to ascertain if the horses were safe. My companions were sound asleep & the horses standing motionless by the trees. Stiff and cold I waited a little & then the slight noise made by living creatures irritated me after being so long on the stretch & I determined to go nearer the lower end of the water & listen there. The night was now so far advanced that success seemed so hopeless that caution was scarcely necessary besides if they were coming I must hear them far enough away to allow ample time to sneak away before they saw me. Musing thus I strolled down by the edge of the water. Was it fog rising from the plain that enveloped me or a mist creeping down from the range? No it was the smell of dust, the wild mob had surprised me & without a whimper or a sound were at hand. Listening intently I felt rather than heard they were at the water's brink & breathlessly I stole back to the camp. A few seconds were sufficient for us to mount & we hastened round the trees to the watering place. To my intense disappointment there was nothing there but the thick dust indicated that they were in flight & I knew it was back to their haunts. No doubt they had heard or smelt me & were racing for the shelter of the forest. Now brave old horse show the metal you are made of. To cut them off from that dense line of timber is the only chance & it will tax your utmost speed and endurance. Away across the rotten plain at full gallop the soft friable soil giving at every hoof beat the splendid old stockhorse ploughed his way without falter or check. Then we gained the firm land & he swept along at the speed of a race horse. Ahead I could hear the crash of breaking boughs as the scrubbers entered the belt of dried timber. Seeing the trail now & keeping to the right out of the dust I could distinguish the last of the mob a few hundred yards in front. Now old horse for a final effort or it will be too late. Thro' the white trunks of the dead mulga, past the straggling tail of the scrubbers we shot with an exultant rush along side the leaders. The dark interlaced bushes were but a few yards in advance but before they could be reached the noble old stockhorse was in front & with a shout of triumph we swung the brutes round. All but one, even in the brief moment when crashing boughs were ringing about my ears I saw a cock horned brindle cow with a large star on her forehead slip behind me into the forest & escape. The rest turned back with furious speed upon the stragglers giving time for the stockman & Jack to come up. Then we forced the reluctant wretches down onto the plain & played with them as it were until daylight broke.

Perhaps none but those who have known the ecstasy of the chase after the wild scrub cattle can understand the impatience with which I waited for the slowly coming dawn, the anxiety to distinguish the forms of the animals so often chased in vain, to see if each & all of the noted leaders were there. One after another they were all recognised. Great raking bullocks, old & wild, fierce bulls with huge shaggy heads among them. Sullen looking & dejected they restlessly roamed about but ever in the backward direction to the mountain. So it was all the way to the yard, resisting every step & horning each other as they kept ringing round as the manner of such lawless animals is when in the toils. Can one wonder, the wild free life is over & whether by

> instinct or reason they doubtless fully realise it. It may sound absurdly sentimental to some but in spite of my interest as a squatter in favour of quiet herds I have never been able to help feeling sorry for the miserable captives. Do not suppose, however, any weakness of the kind prevented me promptly shooting all the ring leaders, indeed the greater number & sending the remainder away to market where they could trouble me no more.
>
> It was a ticklish job getting the brutes to the yards & many were the breaks away particularly of the bulls before that was accomplished. Every care that a long experience could suggest was exercised or some would certainly have got away. Miles distant from the station they were mixed with a quiet milking lot & so inveigled to their destruction.
>
> As for the brindle cow that escaped, weeks afterwards I heard that she joined a small milking mob at a station fifty miles out back & as she bore a brand that stamped her as a scrubber she was incontinently shot for beef.
>
> That's how we broke up the Mt McPherson wild mob of scrubbers.

Simpson's marriage on 12 September 1872 was clearly a turning point in his extraordinary life. He describes in his *Memoirs* the next four years at Marra as 'the happiest in my life'. The loneliness he must have suffered for several years, living in relative isolation, was gone. However, it must have been hard for his twenty-one-year-old schoolteacher wife Jane, from Sydney. His *Memoirs* say surprisingly little about her, nor do they describe her in any detail. However, the extensive regular private correspondence between them when he was away managing the stations seems to indicate that, in his own way, he was devoted to her. Between 1873 and 1880 they had five sons, three of whom spent part of their early years at Marra. Wilcannia, fifty miles away, was the closest town of any size. The horse and paddle steamers (if there was enough water in the river for the latter) were the principal forms of transport, apart from walking. Simpson was away on one of the three runs for much of the time, so there would have been long periods when Jane was separated from him, largely relying on others for support, either at Marra or elsewhere. He was a regular correspondent with her over much of this time, presumably attempting to make up for these long absences.

Simpson's earliest known letter to Jane was in October 1873, a year after their marriage. It reveals something of what life was like for him and also his yearning to be back with her, wherever she was at the time of his writing. It is a pity that the family records do not include responses from her. All of the letters below or parts of them were written in longhand and have thus survived for well over one hundred years. Their content has not been seen, let alone published, before now:

> Woolshed
> October 17/1873
> My own Pet Jennie,
>
> Here we are all my buttons off and never a needle to sow [sic] them on, both elbows out too and not a clean shirt, does much matter tho', things should be in keeping and there is nothing clean about this beastly place. Yesterday it blew a gale, unroofed this dwelling home of mine, filled everything with dust from people's eyes to the camp oven, such a sight of bung eyes, Wark had two in short spaces of time. I heard two also but not of quite such pretensions [sic]. Each fellow one met could not boast an infirmity of vision if he had any at all. How about myself? Well I escaped them all day in the thick of it drafting and herding sheep.

> We have not got on very fast the last two days tho' we worked from daylight to dark so I intend working all tomorrow (Sunday). I can't stand doing nothing now my Jennie is away and a day saved is something …
>
> I have fire branded over 2300 sheep with mine own hand today, so am not in very good order for writing, but could not send to the post tomorrow without a kiss to pet Jennie.
>
> Good night my darling
>
> Yours sincerely
> S Newland

The letters that have survived and been handed down the generations reveal a man of undoubted devotion to Jane, and show his courage, patience, hard work and a will to succeed, irrespective of the circumstances. The age of the letters means that they are no longer easy to read and so inevitably there are gaps. Also it seems that some letters were written after a hard day's work and therefore do not always make complete sense. In a letter to Jane, or Jennie, as he called her, dated 9 November 1873, some days after the birth of their first son Henry, he writes:

> I fear this will be but a poor answer to your letters but I am very busy with accounts as well as epistles ever since returning from Ryans in this office and that was before dinner. You have never seen me work yet, could have but been able to take a peep lately, you would know what a horrid slave a poor devil of a manager is sometimes. I can't answer all your news, must even leave it till we meet and talk it over only with the luck of catching a steamer just leaving Wilcannia and I hope to be with you in three weeks.

The periodic pressures on the relationship between Simpson and Jane must have been significant, given his long absences, the demands on his time, the extent of his responsibilities and his driving will to succeed. The following excerpt from a letter written by him from Marra to Jane in October 1876 at a time when she had left to go to Adelaide, shows both his devotion and his anguish:

> My dear Jennie your perfect trust in us – or rather in me – in leaving the station as you did has touched me much & you have nobly allowed for the only part of our married life I could ever wish had never been. It moved me greatly when you left & since I have thought more of my wife than ever she will perhaps believe. It was very hard upon you leaving us & I almost felt a brute in having it so yet I know it was the best plan & you will never have cause to regret it very likely ever be glad of valuing my love as you do for I am proud of my wife for in consequence of her conduct in this matter.

Simpson's capacity to get on with the task at hand, notwithstanding some human frailties, is revealed time and again in these letters, an example being his letter (in part) to Jane in 1877; he is back at Marra on his own after they had bought their family house, Undelcarra, in Burnside, in the foothills of Adelaide, in late 1876. By then, they had three sons, these being Henry Simpson, born on 3 November 1873, Philip Mesmer, born on 2 February 1875, and Victor Marra, born on 18 August 1876. It is this sort of letter from Simpson that emphasises how unfortunate it is that letters to him that she undoubtedly wrote have not survived:

> Marra
> July 3 1877
> My dearest Jennie
>
> Your three letters of June 7th, 14th & 21st all reached me at Warlo on Saturday last. Katies [Jane's sister] of 14th did also. I

> will answer the dear little woman's nice letter soon. The night I received these mementos of you all I had an intense longing to be back again, could sleep little that night & then dreamt much. Still the work appears to agree with me, had a week almost free from head ache & never felt really tired tho hard at it early too late. I must be in good health too for I never feel the slightest fear or nervousness at anything.

A letter to Jane in mid-July 1877 at Undelcarra shows Simpson's concern for her wellbeing as result of child-bearing, where he wrote:

> You must try and not feel so much alone, believe me I would come if I could. It is better [for you] as it is.
>
> Your faintings show that you are weak & should have a long rest from nursing.

It is little wonder things were difficult for Jane: her husband's long absences and having five children in seven years would be enough to make many women faint! In the latter part of the same letter, he refers to what must have been his problem with headaches:

> A huge box of pills came this post, one to be taken three times a day, only fancy that. However, my head has been better lately until last Sunday when it was a bit bad. I'll try what this stuff does any how.

Simpson's letters to his wife during this difficult time also say surprisingly little about their children when very young. However, these were Victorian times, such as they were, and Simpson appears to have wanted to take part in nurturing and supporting his family notwithstanding the real difficulties of distance and communication. This trait becomes more obvious in his later years when he had more opportunities. He clearly had a strong affinity with the first-born son Henry, which is hardly surprising. Fortunately, a swathe of letters have survived that were written by Simpson to Henry as a young man studying medicine in London. The excerpt below from a letter written to Jane from Marra on 30 October 1873 reflects his fondness for Henry:

> With best love to Jennie and my dear little fellows. Tell Harry his papa sends him a kiss & wants to see his little boy very much.
>
> Goodbye Jennie dear
> Yours sincerely
> S Newland

The second son Philip is little mentioned as a younger man and it appears that the third, Victor, seems to have had some difficulties with his father as a boy when growing up, as is recounted in the chapter devoted to him. By contrast, in later years, Simpson seems to have had an exceptional relationship with his fourth son, Clive, while little is known about the relationship between the father and fifth son Ralph.

A letter written by Simpson in June 1877 gives a great deal of information about Simpson's way of life and includes his reflections upon his activities. By reproducing it in full we are able to glean further understanding of his personality at that time of his busy life:

> Marra
> June 3 1877
> My dearest Jennie,
>
> We arrived here the night before last (Friday) from the M- Shed, came up pleasantly and well. Had two horses (Barney & Nora)

that had never been driven while I was away & tho' a little bother to get in they went splendidly. Yesterday I rode Dandy down on to Warlo where you went with me, to look at the cattle. They are looking well & I intend sending off a mob when I return from the Paroo. Tomorrow we start up there, have all the horses ready now. These runs look splendid, the grass would surprise you. The house and surroundings too are very neat and nice, pleasing me much. I have much enjoyed a talk with dear old Minnie and have not half had enough yet. She looks well but rather thin. I asked her this morning if she would try the cot but can't get a satisfactory answer. You see she talks to me about you all and the subject is a never ending one. I don't know how the six months are to be got over for while here I so much miss the dear faces of my household, perhaps more than since I left. This morning I weighed and only fancy am nine stone 2 pounds in slippers. Indeed am in splendid health, tho' a bit stiff from my long hard ride yesterday. Now you will see the necessity of your getting shiny & fat too or I certainly shall become too young for you. Only be well and happy when I return & we will have a jolly time of it. Pitch anxiety to the ... leave the babies (of course there will be none tho') to the nurse & we can fly round everywhere. I'll lick both you & Katie at archery besides other things. I feel now I would like a good hug & the bed is uncommonly cold to get into these nights. The nippers seemed delighted to see me. Fanny by the by gives ample promise if front development goes for anything. Mr Perks is a sight so untidy, does not seem happy & evidently has not made friends. I saw Barr passing Warlo, he asked after you, the children and 'that other young lady'. He looks well as indeed do all the old hands & both blacks and whites ask after the lot of you by no means forgetting the kids. You can tell Harry I told Fanny he had sent her a kiss. Your next letter will

> reach me at Talyealye. I have arranged for them to be sent on from Wilcannia so you must always direct here. I have had a good deal of writing since arriving besides this is the second after receiving yours. Am going to write to dear little Katie also so you will get about all I have to tell between you. With love to the boys and to yourself dear Jennie.
>
> Yours sincerely
>
> S Newland
> Kind regards to all my friends.

A letter written to Jane in July 1877 explains some of the activities involved in his life as a squatter, mentioning also how he looks forward to seeing his family soon:

> The tailing lambs is not done yet but thus far they give 81 percent. I hoped for better but am satisfied. The weather is now fine & looks more suitable for shearing, & men are so numerous as to be a positive nuisance so there ought to be no difficulty this year. Indeed I anticipate none. If things only go straight I have great hopes of seeing my dear Jennie earlier than we have thought. I hope the boys will go on well now & be fine fellows.

Little did he know then how prophetic that last sentence turned out to be.

Neither Simpson's letters to his wife, nor his reflections in *Memoirs* go into much detail about his family, apart from enquiring about them and confirming that he looks forward to seeing them all again in the letters. Similarly, *Memoirs* contains little information about them and no names even are mentioned. The fourth and fifth sons were born at Simpson and Jane's Adelaide home Undelcarra, more of which is written about in other chapters.

Newland family c. 1885. Philip, Jane (mother) and Henry back row and Clive, Ralph and Victor front row.

In the excerpt relating to Undelcarra from *Memoirs* below, it is made clear that all the sons were expected to be 'men' in the traditional sense, notwithstanding their life of relative privilege:

> Two more sons were born here [at Undelcarra], and it proved an ideal home in which to bring up a family of boys. There was plenty of room for outdoor games and exercise, also timber and water to develop their propensity for work. As they grew older, horses, ponies and vehicles were at their disposal, and

> the training they received fitted them to be self-reliant in their boyhood, and capable in manhood. I have never believed in the pampering of boys: if my sons wanted to ride, they caught their own ponies in the paddocks, and rode them bareback to the stables; if they desired more pocket money, they earned it by doing odd jobs on the place. I learnt my own lessons in life in a hard school and it was my desire that my boys should learn that pleasures must be won, and so to foster in them a sense of responsibility, too often lacking, I fear, when life is made easy for the rising generation.

Despite Simpson having little to say in his *Memoirs* about his sons, that he clearly expected them to be men in the traditional sense is apparent in the final and somewhat revealing statement about them in the last section of that book:

> Five sons were born to us, two are tragically dead [Ralph died in 1933 after publication of Simpson's *Memoirs*] but all have played their part in work and sport, in peace and war.

The chapters on each of the sons describe their activities and attempts to show how the lives of each – where information is still available – fulfilled their father's expectations of them.

In Simpson's occasional references to the children in his letters written from Marra and other locations in New South Wales he singles out his oldest son Henry, or Harry as he was called. An example is given in a letter written to Jane on 3 July 1877:

> My dear little boy Harry, so he wants to send me 'lollies'. You must get him some & say this then to him & tell him to give Bob some & baby [presumably Philip] if he may have any. I hope now you have weaned the baby your weakness will pass off & more than all the old strength come back.

Undelcarra c. 1900

The last sentence above indicates Simpson's concern for Jane's welfare, expressed regularly in his letters. This is not surprising, given his long absences away at Marra and the other stations. She was often pregnant during these times, as well as having other young children to care for. It was fortunate that she had a nurse to assist her. A paragraph from a letter in July 1877 again demonstrates Simpson's concerns:

> I do hope my pet you will now be at ease & get strong. You really must not worry. This is the one thing that troubles me now, if you don't give yourself a chance of regaining strength what is the good of my going away at all. With health the future looks so bright that for both our sakes nothing should be left undone that can be done to gain that. I am sorry to hear that the baby is sick but don't fret about it. I do often wish I could see your old girlish spirits back again. But there, I won't preach anymore.

As there is nothing from Jane herself in the collection of letters held by the Newland family, it is difficult to know exactly what she thought of her circumstances. It is reasonable to assume that Jane found her early married life trying, given Simpson's long absences from home, either from Marra when they lived there, or later when she was at Undelcarra in South Australia and he was seven hundred miles away managing the stations in western New South Wales. While we know that she had a nurse to assist her and that her sister Kate appears to have spent time with her, it would nevertheless have been a lonely existence. With five sons born between 1873 and 1880 – one child every sixteen or so months – it must have been incredibly hard work for her. It is thus not surprising that Simpson's letters refer to her health being less than robust over this period. Generously, Jane seemed to have concerns about Simpson, even though he clearly appears to be doing what he wanted in managing his stations proficiently and accumulating a great deal of wealth. The letter that follows was written by him to Jane after the first three sons were born:

> Marra
> Sept 24 1877
> My dearest Jennie
>
> Last Friday night I arrived in from the Paroo, having left the sheep at Scriveners & ridden on in two days, rather hard on my old bones. I sent Stuart & others on the next day to meet the sheep for they are more troublesome than I ever saw stock in my life. The week I was with them they knocked us all up but more bother when I left having got on to good feed. I was indeed glad to get in & receive news of my dear ones. One of your letters would have alarmed me but as it was very late on Friday night & on Saturday morning I got one of a reassuring tenor there was not

> much time for uneasiness. It is a dreadful thing the sad end of Charles Butler but my pet that is no reason for you to feel more anxious about me. I am just as safe as before and shall endeavour to take care of my life for the sake of us all. Be happy Jennie dear I am where I ought to be while there is so much to do & I retain the management of the stations. I could not without feeling shame leave now & that I know you would not wish. Still not a day shall be lost when I can turn my face homeward. My darling not even you can more ardently long for that time than I do but I try to keep it down. I think it is the longest separation we shall ever have & life will be none the less sweet when it is over & we can both feel we have done well.

To this point, the account of Simpson's extraordinary life and his reflections have largely covered the establishment of himself at Marra and his home, family and work life – insofar as the small amount of material available has permitted. But Simpson's story is much more than this: in middle age he also became deeply involved in a number of number of important issues and activities, remaining committed to them until his death. For the purposes of this account, I have selected those I think would have resonated most with his sons and, more remarkably, are still important today – each perhaps deserves a full chapter, given their relevance over 140 years later. For simplicity I have categorised these areas of interest as: Aborigines, writing, politics, the Murray River, the Northern Territory, the North–South Railway, and public institutional involvement. Each is addressed in a way that attempts to add to the character and nature of Simpson's personality and how that personality was moulded by his circumstances. None of these subjects is straightforward but his involvement in each serves to highlight the underlying theme of the development of self-reliant and worthy men – for him and for his children.

Aboriginal people

In relation to the Indigenous people, it is important to keep in mind that Simpson arrived in South Australia in 1839, around fifty years after Europeans first seriously attempted to settle in Australia and three years after the first European arrival in the colony of South Australia. Various attempts were made by the first European settlers to recognise Indigenous culture and to respect their legitimate rights and Chapter 1 mentions the Letters Patent, which refer to, among other things, how the Aboriginal people should be treated in South Australia. While the ideals may have been stated, the reality was different. This is no great surprise, given the difficulties, both perceived and real, for the new colony.

Simpson is credited as being one of the early pioneers who made a serious attempt to consider the country's first inhabitants, notwithstanding the views and behaviour of others. In his foreword to Simpson's *Memoirs*, Sir Langdon Bonython asserts: 'the finest tribute to the character of Mr Newland is to be found in his relations with the aboriginal natives'.

In his *Memoirs* Simpson devotes a full chapter to native tribes and types and clearly recognises:

> the detested interloper [Europeans] tak[ing] possession of all his country, after slaughtering many of his people in their vain attempts at resistance, making shepherds and stockmen of the free hunters, then later to see them wither and die.

While there is no indication that Simpson committed overt acts of aggression against Aboriginal people, the dispossession of which he was unwittingly involved as a squatter does not mean he escapes direct or indirect complicity in the transgression of their rights, at least in part. His books refer to clashes with Aboriginal tribes in various ways, particularly in overlanding stock through what he described as hostile Aboriginal territory. It is difficult to believe that he did not see and possibly participate in such clashes, in instances where protection of his property was a priority for him. In *Memoirs* the following passage reveals something of the pioneer's dilemma:

> Unquestionably pioneering was fraught with many difficulties, demanding every ounce of energy and thought. A stern outlook was engendered, perhaps, by combatting opposing forces, and the successful raising of cattle and sheep in a country likely to be stricken by drought or flood at any time. The risks, too, of sending animals to market, as well as keeping them free from the ravages of disease and wild dogs, the task of securing suitable help and of dealing justly with the dispossessed natives combined with the necessity of maintaining law and order in a country practically destitute of Government aid, were a few of the trials that beset the early occupant of the outback spaces. Grim realities had often to be faced and quick decisions made – decisions that were sometimes far-reaching in their effects for good or evil.

Given these circumstances and given the stated imperative to consolidate the British Empire in the Victorian era, it is scarcely believable that Simpson did not indeed witness and was not aware of issues and events relating to Aboriginal people that perhaps might have concerned him, and nowadays would shock and anger most people. Yet at the time such actions and events may have been regarded as expedient and possibly acceptable by many.

It is difficult not to be judgmental about the early settlers' behaviour; it is equally difficult to appreciate the circumstances, risks, loneliness and aspirations for success, as well the task of managing to survive – and then having to live with one's conscience. Today, more than a century and a half after these events, we are not confronted by the challenges the settlers had to face in their daily lives. Whether the consciences of those whose actions impacted adversely on Indigenous people troubled them is something we may never know.

No one is suggesting that Simpson and his contemporaries should be absolved of any wrongdoing; merely that these are complex issues that would have tested any person. The record shows he made considerable effort to behave responsibly towards Aboriginal people and that he also tried to understand a culture that was acknowledged and even recognised by so few at that time is to his credit. In his efforts to understand Aboriginal people he clearly stood out from others and this may have had underlying negative implications for him with some of his peers who did not share his views.

Writing

Simpson's efforts as an author have left a more than interesting legacy, although some might consider that his writings raise more questions about him than they answer. Of his books, *Memoirs of Simpson Newland CMG*, with its somewhat understated approach, reveals much of great interest, particularly from an historical perspective, about an astonishing life of sheer tenacity and outstanding achievement. Yet it is much more than that. Aside from the more personal aspects, which constitute a minor part, this book chronicles a series of events, some of which are extraordinarily relevant, even today. The chapters on subjects such as the Murray River, the North–South Railway and Indigenous people are matters of current national policy interest, while information on venerable and much-admired institutions such as the Wyatt Benevolent Trust and the Royal Zoological Society of SA is more relevant and important to South Australians. Clearly there was much that Simpson wanted to share with others and *Memoirs* successfully apprises the reader of the facts relating to these issues.

The first of his books, the novel *Paving the Way*, is the best known of his writings and is described by him as a romance of the Australian bush. When asked about the veracity of the story, he is alleged to have said that all of it is true – and none of it. It certainly seems to be an account of an extraordinary set of circumstances, some parts of which seem to be based on personal experiences and augmented with vivid embellishments.

The second of his books, *Blood Tracks of the Bush* is a strange mixture of the macabre and the fantastic. In both books, the Australian bush and the vastness of a continent largely uninhabited by Europeans and not subject to the European tenets of law as many now know it emerge as common themes. In both, Aborigines are key characters and the troubled relationship between 'blacks and whites' is a regular and sometimes disturbing theme. Also by Simpson's admission, both these books are likely to be based on aspects of his life. If that is indeed true, it adds further to the complexities of Simpson's life experience. What did he see and participate in?

These books demonstrate relatively enlightened social views for the time; by contrast, it is reasonable to question his role in some of the episodes involving great violence and other atrocities. Simpson rightly makes the point that the life of a pioneer is fraught with difficulty and that the individual is inevitably confronted by events that require a decision about self-preservation, possibly at the expense of someone else's life.

In such an astonishing life, he would have had to live with his conscience and perhaps questioned, even possibly regretted, some of the activities in which he may have participated. These are questions about which we can but speculate.

Simpson's short stories are an interesting mixture. The one reproduced in full in this chapter is defined by a strong 'bush flavour' and aptly reflects the underlying theme of this book: men should behave like men and demonstrate manly characteristics. On the other hand, 'The Squatter and the Girl', written as a largely unknown and forgotten short story, was published in the *Adelaide Observer* on Saturday 15 December 1900. It is something of a 'Wuthering Heights' style of story of unrequited love and loss set in Victoria and New South Wales, with a bush setting very familiar to the author; in fact, the action takes place where Simpson lived for much of his bush life as a squatter. The motivation for his writing this story is intriguing, since it certainly appears that part of it reflects some of his own experiences, particularly with the bush setting and possibly with women. One cannot help but note that his own wife Jane was eighteen years his junior – as was one of the story's characters – when he married her at the height of his squatting period in New South Wales.

Other short stories such as 'Old Time Memories – a Band of Pioneers', written for the *South Australian Register* in 1895, the unpublished 'Killarney', 'Marseilles to Pt Said' (1890) and 'A Trip to Carlsbad' (around 1900) are more factual accounts of his own travel experiences. Yet each is an interesting work in itself and shows Simpson's strong desire to record his experiences and his perceptions of the circumstances in which he found himself. 'Old Time Memories' in particular reveals the author's sense of humour, his ability to laugh at himself and his capacity to be self-effacing; a sense of humility comes through strongly. However, the characteristic is certainly not reflected in Roland Grantley, the somewhat pompous and aloof hero of his first book, *Paving the Way.*

This variety in his written offerings adds to the complexity of Simpson's character. He seemed to want to make a mark in the history of Australia, but not in a way that might impart any sense of arrogance or self-aggrandisement. He would not have wished for this, nor would he have wished for his sons to behave similarly. Yet the sons' stories, where known, indicate that they achieved a great deal, of which any parents, including Simpson and Jane, would have been proud.

Politics

One hundred and fifty years or so years ago the nature of political life and the life of politicians was very different from that of today. Politics, as we know it now, has for some time been a career where politicians are relatively well paid, and a great deal is expected of them as a result, although this does not necessarily translate into today's politicians being better or more motivated than their predecessors. Indeed, it could be argued that the political process is much less 'honourable' than it was previously. The types of people who became politicians in the beginning of the twenty-first century are generally very different from those who became involved in politics in the latter part of the nineteenth century. At that time individuals were asked to run for office because they were considered to be people who had the potential to contribute to 'the common good'. This criterion is not necessarily one that applies in the twenty-first century, with the requirements of political parties and factional alignments.

In his *Memoirs*, Simpson refers several times to periods of solitude, when he was alone at Marra, or on one of his many long rides on horseback in the Australian outback. Clearly he was a thinker, and he recognised there were areas in this developing country to which he thought he could contribute. He also wanted to see Australia, and South Australia in particular, develop and become places of note. *Memoirs* refers to wanting to fulfil a long-held wish to enter public life, not least because of the opportunities he saw in relation to the Murray River and the Northern Territory. His contemporaries seemed to encourage him to do so.

Simpson's time in politics was relatively short, notwithstanding that he occupied a senior Cabinet position for a couple of years. Unlike the actions of many of today's politicians, in 1885 he resigned as the South Australian Treasurer because he thought others may do a better job, given the then difficult financial circumstances facing South Australia, and for health reasons. His political career began in 1881 and lasted for about six years.

Murray River

We can only conjecture what Simpson would think of the current debate about the Murray River, the principal component of the Murray–Darling Basin. His knowledge, particularly of these river systems, had been developed over a long period. Initially as a boy and young man, he became very familiar with the unregulated lower Murray and lakes into which the Coorong discharges. He later lived on the Darling at Marra and other properties in the Murray–Darling Basin. His many trips on river steamers, as well as his droving of stock, both sheep and cattle, from Marra to points up and downstream, including all the way to Adelaide, taught him a great deal about the river system, as it was then. A droving trip of the likes of Adelaide to Marra, which he undertook several times, would take at least six weeks, across almost entirely trackless country, but nevertheless requiring considerable bush skill and highly developed stockmanship. His vision of the Murray–Darling as a regulated and navigable transport highway using paddle steamers was sensible and relevant for its time. The then-unregulated nature of those rivers meant that he and others had to contend with massive floods and unforgiving droughts. His pastoral interests in the upper reaches of the Paroo River clearly gave him a perspective beyond purely the Murray and the Darling. His *Memoirs* refer to a:

> system of locking and conservation, by construction of extensive reservoirs was looked upon as the means of fulfilling the great possibilities of the mighty river – to open up the broad Riverina for irrigation, and to provide direct transport to the markets of the world for its products.

Given the debate currently between the states and the Commonwealth on the best management practices for the Murray–Darling Basin by means of a plan agreed between the various state jurisdictions and the Commonwealth, it is notable to reflect on the following excerpt from *Memoirs*:

> Somehow as time went on the national spirit of the people changed, and the petty rivalries between the colonies as to how much water each was entitled to use hampered progress, and thus it came about that Victoria and New South Wales entered into large schemes of diverting the waters of the Murray and its tributaries. Several active associations were formed in various settled parts of the Riverina country to protect the interests of navigation, and meanwhile successive Governments of South Australia played ignominious parts, spending years attending useless conferences, discussing and wrangling with our sister

> States over the division of water calculated to flow for given periods through certain gauges. So far as New South Wales and Victoria were concerned, the true object of these conferences was to discover how little South Australia could be induced to accept, and to gain time to push on with their own works.

Chris Guest's recent *Sharing the Water – One hundred years of River Murray politics* notes that each state conducted its own royal commission on the river between 1884 and 1887.[7] A meeting in Corowa in 1902 involving the prime minister of the new Commonwealth agreed to appoint an Interstate Royal Commission to comprehensively investigate the conservation and distribution of the waters of the Murray River and its tributaries. At this commission, the justice of South Australia's claim to full riparian rights in the Murray was put (given that most the water-yielding catchments are in New South Wales and Victoria), along with a proposal to construct locks and weirs along the river in the interests of irrigation and navigation. This proposal was accepted and the River Murray League, predecessor to the Murray–Darling Basin Association, was formed on 10 June 1902, with G. Brookman, MLC, as president and Simpson Newland and the Hon. J.L. Parsons as vice-presidents. Simpson became president of this association in 1904 at a time of considerable conflict with the upstream states: a further Royal Commission was proposed, legal proceedings between South Australia and Victoria were threatened and various premiers' conferences were held. Simpson, then in his mid- to late-seventies, was involved in all of these. He was clearly frustrated by the Murray question not being taken seriously enough and was deeply committed to further expansion of transport by river, a decent outlet at the Murray Mouth and an export port at Victor Harbor. He probably never contemplated the current problems of over-diversion of the basin's waters.

Simpson's views at that time appeared to reflect the thinking of the day; yet the advent of railways and the hazards of vessels of any size passing through the Murray Mouth appear not to have been apparent to him, which is surprising in light of his recognition of the importance of railways to the state, as described below. All of this work, including his involvement, culminated in 1914 in the River Murray Waters Agreement and the establishment of the River Murray Commission. It is likely that the controversy over waters of the Murray–Darling Basin over one hundred years ago will continue for many years yet and indeed may intensify. The role of the now Murray–Darling Basin Authority has a long life ahead of it.

Northern Territory and the North-South railway

Simpson strongly supported the Northern Territory remaining as part of South Australia. He advocated for over a period of well over twenty years for South Australia to have the benefit of the territory's natural resources, as he saw them. The Northern Territory was annexed to South Australia by the Imperial Government in 1863, even though, according to Ross Duncan,[8] much of the early exploration of the territory was initiated from Queensland. One plan was to allocate the land north of the Tropic of Capricorn to Queensland and the southern portion to South Australia. The Queensland Government declined this offer, whereas in 1859 the South Australian Governor, Sir Richard McDonnell, asked the Colonial Office in London to extend South Australia's northern border to the Arafura Sea following the opening up of a north–south track by explorer John McDouall Stuart in 1862.

While this suggestion was not supported at that time, it was eventually accepted on the basis that taking stock northerly by such a route made more sense and was easier than stock being moved westerly from Queensland. Railways became a key form of transport during Simpson's time in those places without rivers. Along with the annexation of the Northern Territory, Simpson, as a Member of the South Australian Parliament, proposed that the cost of the North–South railway (of seven million pounds) be met through a land grant system involving the private sector. In August 1886, he was successful in gaining parliamentary approval for a commission to be established to consider the proposal. The commission was charged by Governor Sir William Robinson to consider four questions:

1. That it is expedient that the Transcontinental Railway should be forthwith continued from its present terminus in South Australia proper to Pine Creek in the Northern Territory;
2. That it is expedient that the same should be constructed by private enterprise;
3. That in order to induce capitalists to undertake such construction, concessions of land either on alternate blocks or otherwise should be offered, and to such an extent as may be agreed upon by the Legislature;
4. That such further terms, limitations, restrictions and obligations as may be necessary should be imposed.

The commission was appointed on 26 January 1887 and was made up of David Murray, MLC, John Cockburn, MP, Richard Baker, GMG, MLC, Allan Campbell, MLC, Thomas Burgoyne, MP, Simpson Newland, MP, and Martin Basedow, MP. Sitting over a period of twelve months, it examined twenty-six witnesses, including Charles Todd, CMG (Postmaster-General), George

Goyder (Suryeyor-General), the explorers C. Giles and David Lindsay, and Simpson Newland himself.

The commission held its first meeting on 2 February 1887. Simpson, who was then aged fifty-three, was elected chairman at the first meeting and early discussion focused on the nature and pastoral potential of the country in far north South Australia, between Strangways Springs and The Peake. Not surprisingly, Simpson advised his fellow commissioners of his intention to personally examine part of the proposed route for the railway. He did so on horseback, travelling to Alice Springs and through the adjoining country, in company with a local station manager and an Aboriginal man, whose name sadly was not part of the recorded proceedings.

A reading of the commission report indicates that witnesses examined had varying views about the worth of the proposal. Engineers saw no issues with constructing the line along the route proposed. However, difficulties were anticipated with water quality for steam engines, white ant attack on the wooden sleepers and a lack of local timber for the sleepers themselves. Todd considered that the railway would be 'of slight use' in conveying mail to Great Britain, while Goyder thought it may lead to better stock management during droughts, in that stock could be moved out of areas quickly by train rather than by droving, where horses were used. Simpson's own evidence reflected his extensive bush knowledge and his pastoralist proclivities. His very real interest in the country, its vegetation and wildlife and principally its capacity to generate wealth from pastoralism and mining emerged strongly in his written evidence, available in Parliamentary Papers for South Australia.

When the final commission report was submitted to the South Australian Parliament on 26 January 1887, it recommended that the railway be extended through to Pine Creek (from Angle Pole, on the overland telegraph near Oodnadatta) using the land grant system to fund it. It was to be completed in seven years from the signing of the contract, and not more than one-third of the land fronting the railway was to be conceded to the construction contractor. Eighteen conditions were stipulated for any potential contractor.

Not surprisingly, the proposal foundered, given its cost and given the varying degrees of enthusiasm at the time about its value to South Australia. The Northern Territory was clearly a burden on the State Treasury and existing and future returns of revenue were assessed to be doubtful. Simpson remained a strong advocate for the proposal until his death, believing the Northern Territory to be a source of great future mining and pastoral wealth. He also believed that South Australia, with the Northern Territory as part of its jurisdiction after Federation in 1901, would make South Australia the premier state. Without the territory in his reasoned opinion, South Australia would have less importance than the other states. Indeed Simpson was passionate enough about the railway proposal to fund a trip to London for himself in 1906 at the age of seventy-two to attempt to raise capital for the venture.

A change of government in South Australia, followed by delays, the reversion of the Northern Territory to the Commonwealth in 1910, and later the onset of the First World War, served to scuttle the proposal. More than one hundred years later, a railway has been built to connect Adelaide with Darwin, although some have argued that it was a poor and unnecessary investment. Undoubtedly, Simpson would be pleased that the proposal eventually came to fruition, although the reasons for its construction at the beginning of the twenty-first century, as distinct from the end of the nineteenth century, when he was such a strong advocate, are quite different. It is also notable that in 2017 the South Australian Government stated publicly that it was interested in exploring cooperative ventures with the government of the Northern Territory. A change of government twelve months later may mean a change to potential cooperation.

Public institutions

The evidence shows that Simpson wasn't a person to accumulate wealth for his benefit alone. He had a well-developed sense of community service and public duty, as his somewhat reluctant entry into politics at a difficult time in South Australia's history confirms. His wide interests led to his involvement in various institutions. He was a foundation member of the Geographical Society of Australasia (SA Branch) in 1885 (later the Royal Geographical Society, SA Branch), of which he was elected president in 1895, a role he held three times over the subsequent decade or more. His papers covered topics such as Aborigines, *The Parkengees or Aboriginal Tribes on the Darling River*, published in 1887, while his wide-ranging president's address in 1898 looked at Antarctic exploration, ethnology and anthropology, Australian exploration, the Calvert expedition, statues for Elder and Stuart and the protection of native fauna. He was president in 1902 when the Flinders Column at Mt Lofty summit, often known as the Obelisk, was so named by Governor Lord Tennyson in honour of the explorer Matthew Flinders.

In 1892, Simpson joined the Zoological and Acclimatisation Society, now known as the Royal Zoological Society of SA, becoming its president in 1906, a position he held for over a decade. Interestingly, in light of the later establishment of Monarto Open Range Zoo, unsuccessful attempts were made during his presidency to buy land adjacent to the Murray River for grazing native and imported animals. Also during his presidency a scheme was negotiated with the Adelaide City Council to expand the Adelaide Zoo by leasing land adjacent to the current Zoo across the River Torrens, upon condition it be properly fenced and a bridge be constructed over the river. While the fence was erected, insufficient money was raised for the proposed bridge. For his efforts over many years, Simpson was elected an honorary life member of the society in 1922.

In addition to his involvement in these public institutions, in 1895, Simpson, through his friendship with Dr William Wyatt, became a member of the Board of Governors of the Wyatt Benevolent Trust. He was elected chairman in 1900. This society had as its principal object offering assistance to educated people in needy circumstances. Simpson held the position of chairman for twenty-three years. By that time, 230 people were receiving benefits, with £60,000 having been dispensed since the organisation's inception. Simpson's *Memoirs* records the following statement, which is a testament to his desire to help those less fortunate than himself and clearly represents the values that he aspired to and likely expected of his sons. His eldest son Henry subsequently became a chairman, like his father before him:

> It is certain, therefore, that the institution will continue (which it has from strength to strength) to perpetuate the memory of its generous founders, while in the hearts of many men and women warm and grateful thankfulness will bless them for the comfort and help they have provided.

Simpson was made a Companion of the Order of St Michael and St George (CMG) in 1922. He is recorded as having said: 'I was ambitious, but for me, like my father before me, the cause was always greater than the man behind the cause'. His whole-page obituary in *The Observer* of 4 July 1925 described him, among other things, as an esteemed and valuable colonist.

This account of Simpson, the remarkable father of five sons, has attempted to describe a complex and relatively private character, who by his deeds must have left a strong impression on those sons. These events arguably help to explain the strength and achievements of his sons and prompts speculation on how much more there would be to tell if all five sons, rather than just two, had lived to old age.

It is also fitting that the following poem of unknown origin and authorship, located through research by his great granddaughter Elizabeth Stafford (née Newland) in November 2013, be included here. Simpson's remains lie in the Victor Harbor cemetery, with a fine view over the land of his upbringing:

Upon the hilltop by the sea
They laid the pioneer.
Old Simpson Newland, splendid man.
Who held this country dear.
He knew the granite-crested Bluff
When whalers plied their trade.
And through the four score crowded years
He saw great changes made.

The last paragraphs of this chapter on Simpson Newland and his philosophy towards life are best given by him himself. When researching material for this book, I came across the following written by Simpson in pencil in a 'Graphic' black exercise book. The other topics in the exercise book point to its having been written in about 1923, two years before his death. These words, to my knowledge, have remained in the private domain until now:

Life without aims and objects would be mere existence and even though failure to attain all necessarily brings disappointment, it is certainly better to have failed than never to have tried. Even to have advanced a worthy cause one step is not to have lived in vain. Needless to say, bitter thoughts come easily to my mind when I review my failures, for success has been so near and the turning point decided by comparatively trivial events.

There are many problems for the people of this vast continent to solve. One of the greatest, perhaps, is how to people the empty spaces and to prevent the population from clinging to the cities. To allow the capitals to be falsely enriched at the expense of the country is a great mistake foreboding trouble and danger to Australia.

I wonder if any man is wholly satisfied with his life when he reviews his accomplishments. Tinged with my disappointments are bitter thoughts – for I realise how slender has been the thread that decided the issues upon which so much depended. For over forty years I have striven to accomplish the two great things that would have brought inestimable advantages to not only Sth Aus but to the whole continent. I have tried by every means in my power to make people see what I see and to decide these great questions as I believe they should be decided. In my boyhood and early manhood I realised the wonderful possibilities of the River Murray with its network of tributaries and followed with the greatest interest the construction of the overland telegraph to Port Darwin. To bring to maturity the aims of those responsible for the carrying out of this great undertaking was my next great ideal. While still a young man, I decided that I would enter Parliament when I had the opportunity if for no other reason than to help forward these projects.

Hope is still live within me and I feel the day will come when these things will be done; but it's a great pity that so much valuable time has been lost and so much effort to bring about such obvious advantages. Australia offers immense scope for energy, enterprise and unselfish work, for her problems are not easy to solve. Perhaps the most important of these questions is how to populate the immense areas now lying idle and how to prevent people from clinging to the cities. To my mind the only practical remedy is to open up the country and offer facilities to induce people to undertake the hard and risky work of taming the wilderness. Following upon the connection of the railway terminus at Oodnadatta and Pine Creek, a great movement towards Central Australia must result.

4

Five Newland sons

The title of this book indicates that the narrative chiefly concerns the five sons of Simpson Newland, although describing their immediate ancestors is important, especially since I believe that the characters of the five Newland sons were moulded early in their lives by their parents in conjunction with the circumstances in which they lived these lives. In this age of gender equality, inclusion in a book title of the words 'the making of men' is almost to invite allegations of sexist and inappropriate language! I hope what follows will stand on its merits and that the contents and deeds of these men will aptly justify the use of such a title.

It is intriguing that, of the five sons of Simpson and Jane, the fourth, Clive, unlike his brothers, was not given a second name. All of the others received their second names from obscure past relatives, even if the spelling of these names was not always true to the original. Victor was the exception, with his second name being 'Marra'. Because of the name's association with a prominent part of his father's life, it was likely to have been seen by his parents as worthy of recording both for then and for the future. Simpson himself did not have a second name and neither did his brothers or half-brothers. It begs the question of why the fourth son Clive was not baptised with, for example, his mother's maiden name Layton as his second name, which today would seem appropriate.

Given that only two of the five sons lived beyond middle age, coupled with the small amount of material available from family members, this account of the lives of the five sons is largely confined to the first part of the twentieth century. As far as sons Henry and Victor are concerned, more material relating to them is available and some incidents beyond the 1940s have been included where these add to the overall picture I have attempted to paint of these men. Certainly Victor, and to a lesser extent Henry, as with their father before them, would be astonished that a light is being shone upon them in the early part of the third millennium.

Simpson, the sickly child, described in Chapter 2, who became a giant of a man, notwithstanding his diminutive size, and his wife Jane Isabella produced those five sons over a period of seven years. The first three sons spent part of their early lives at Marra station, several kilometres downstream from Tilpa on the Darling River in New South Wales. As I have described, given the isolation and limited support facilities, conditions at that location were quite primitive and therefore risky. The second and third sons, Philip and Victor, were born in western New South Wales, with Victor known to have been born at Marra or thereabouts in 1876, when his mother was in her mid-twenties. The nearby town of Tilpa had been established the year before, meaning that at the time of the birth of these sons there was little by way of a formal town settlement. The dangerous nature of the locality can be appreciated by the fact that the well-known bushranger Captain Starlight had been in the district just seven years earlier, holding up several stations, including Buckanbe and Marra, prior to his eventual capture in late 1868.

The two younger sons, Clive and Ralph, were born in very different circumstances at Undelcarra in Burnside, a substantial family mansion in the foothills of eastern Adelaide. They and their older brothers were fortunate to spend their early years in what might be considered a privileged existence, a beautiful setting and with domestic help.

When Simpson bought Undelcarra from a Mr Debney, a cabinet-maker who had worked on the old Parliament House in North Terrace, it was a single-story house. Simpson and Jane made considerable changes to it, with their efforts transforming it into a grand mansion, which it still is – with a dining room that seats twenty people in comfort and a billiard room – as the photograph shows. A newspaper article about the entertaining undertaken by the Newlands has survived.[9] The article is of great interest to the present owners Antony and Mary Lou Simpson, who were keen to discover as much as possible of the great mansion's history, including its early occupation. The newspaper article describes a pre-wedding tea party for Henry and his wife-to-be Ellen, or Nell:

Undelcarra pre wedding afternoon tea party

August 31, 1910

'Undelcarra' was looking its best on Thursday afternoon, August 27, when Mrs Simpson Newland entertained a large number of friends. The day was a charming one, bright and sunny, and the garden looked very lovely, with quantities of daffodils everywhere, and other spring flowers. The creek, like a small river, running through the garden under its many rustic bridges, made the air full of music, vieing [*sic*] with the string bands discoursing sweet strains from the balcony. Mrs Newland received the guests in the drawing-room, looking very handsome in a black and white toilette with a hat to correspond. Afternoon tea was served in the dining-room, which was beautifully decorated with daffodils and violets. Small tables were also laid out on the verandah. Amongst the guests were Lady Way, in a black costume. Mrs Edward Hawker, electric blue surah, large black hat and feathers. Mrs Walter Duffield in a smart coat and skirt made of mole-coloured velvet; hat and boa to match. Miss Mort (Sydney), grey, with grey torque. Mrs Hart, black bonnet, with violets. Miss Marian Hart wore green voile, tuscan hat with green ribbon and violets, and contributed very much to the success of the afternoon with her sweet singing.

Other guests were the bride, Mrs Hal. Newland, looking charming in a pale blue dress; vieux rose hat. Mrs Clive Newland looked pretty in brown wool crepe de chine; violet scarf and hat. Mrs Mara Newland (South Africa) looked very sweet in a cream dress and scarf and large becoming hat. Mrs Seymour Hawker, cream hat with blue and pink roses. Mrs Alec McCulloch, reseda green, with black hat. Mrs James Gosse, cream coat and skirt; black beaver hat with white plumes. Miss Kathleen Phillips in a smart pink dress with black hat and scarf. Miss Nina Boothby, looked exceedingly well in saxe blue with hat en suite. Mrs A.A. Hamilton, in a becoming shade of heliotrope, with hat to match. Miss Addie Ringwood, black and grey check coat and skirt; smart black hat swathed in wine-coloured silk. Miss Cynthia Hawkes looked well in blue; large black crinoline hat with black velvet and roses. Miss Audrey Jessop, green velvet coat and skirt; black hat. Mrs Leonard Bakewell looked well in grey. Mrs Coghlan wore black, relieved with white. Miss Ada Coghlan wore a blue costume, with hat to match. Mrs C.H.T. Connor, in black. Miss Louise Connor, grey, with black hat and feathers. Other guests were: Mrs Humphrey Marten, Miss Roland, Miss Rachel Luxmore,

Miss deCourcey Connor, Miss Horn, Mrs Eversley Thomas, Mrs Grundy, Miss Florence Young, Mrs Arthur Waterhouse, Mrs Peter Waite, Mrs George Dean.

At Undelcarra, c. 1900. Seated, from left: Clive, Henry, Ralph, Victor and Philip. The identities of the young women and man in the back row are unknown.

The photograph shown above is one of the many unlabelled photos taken between 1904 and 1915 contained in an album belonging to my grandfather Ralph Newland, the youngest son of Simpson and Jane. It shows a group of five young men sitting in the front row, from the viewer's left, Clive, Henry, Ralph, Victor and Philip, with five young women standing behind them and another young man apparently perched on a stool. The photo demonstrates the sort of lives that these young men were probably leading before making their own way in a world outside Adelaide – as expected by their parents, particularly their father. In the photograph, the boys, with their relaxed poses and their casual clothes, seem to be displaying a nonchalant, happy-go-lucky attitude. It's a pity that the photograph's location is unknown, as is the identity of the young women and their connection to the young men; having this information would have been useful.

As I've already indicated, of the five sons, considerable information survives in the hands of family members about the first son Henry and the third son Victor, particularly about their lives and deeds both through public records and existing detailed family records, many still held privately. Letter writing was the prime form of communication at this time in history. Certainly Henry and Victor, along with their mother and father, proved themselves to be regular correspondents. Furthermore, Victor (or Mick as he was called for those who knew him well) kept a journal of his time in Africa.[10] Both his diary and his letters reveal much about him and his personality, certainly more than is available for his four brothers.

In addition, a biographical account of Victor's life in South and British East Africa and based on his journal was prepared by the late Canon A.L. Bulbeck, rector of Christ Church, North Adelaide, where Victor was a parishioner and regular attendee on his return to Adelaide. This account, entitled 'Marra, or Still Paving the Way', was completed in 1963 and has been an important source of information. The detail contained in my account of aspects of Victor's life, especially his time in South and East Africa, is drawn from his journal, much of which is also given in Bulbeck's account. This biography, along with his letters, is revealing and was of great assistance in gaining a better understanding of the measure of this third son of Simpson and Jane's and particularly how his parents moulded his character and strong sense of purpose, albeit from South Australia while he was living in Africa.

The lives of the two sons Henry and Victor, especially as younger men, are marked by actions and achievements that reflect inherited or taught courage, fearlessness, astonishing risk taking and selflessness. If Simpson, the father, had hoped for sons who reflected his view of the world and behaved accordingly, he certainly achieved it with these two sons, as the accounts of their lives clearly demonstrate. While there is some evidence that Simpson was both firm and determined, and perhaps even penny-pinching in situations where he thought necessary, the letters used in this book and held by the family indicate that this is not an entirely accurate assessment of his character. Undoubtedly Simpson was a hard taskmaster and often uncompromising and he had a clear expectation that all of his sons demonstrate the strength of character he had instilled in them. His letters do not support that he was ungenerous; in fact, where he thought it justified, financial support was forthcoming. While it is not widely accepted that Simpson and Jane were generous to their sons, the couple may well have expected their sons to make their own way in the world – that their sons should not assume they were entitled to the couple's wealth. They were happy to be generous if they thought the recipients were deserving.

Of the other three sons, Philip, Clive and Ralph, much less is known, with few family records and little information about their achievements, given their relatively short lives. From the information we have, we can assume that they were likely to have been similar to Victor and Henry. Both the second son Philip and the fourth son Clive died in their early forties in tragic and, in Clive's case, shocking circumstances, which was undoubtedly difficult for their parents, their wives, siblings and children.

My grandfather Ralph, the youngest of the sons, also died relatively young, in his early fifties. Records relating to his life are surprisingly scarce, although some facts previously unknown about him have surfaced during my research. My first cousins and I have been supplied with very little information by Ralph's sons (our fathers) for reasons that are obscure and not understood by any of us. There is no suggestion of mystery, although some might think there is a hint of scandal, as the chapter on Ralph explains.

The early deaths of Philip, Clive and Ralph are likely to be a major explanation for the paucity of retained information about them. Since we know that both Henry and Victor were regular correspondents with their parents and vice versa, it seems likely that Philip, Clive and Ralph were also reasonable correspondents, at least with their parents. Two or three of Clive's letters do survive in the State Library of South Australia from the time when he was in London undertaking postgraduate hospital work as a medical intern, but that is all. Aside from this, nothing has been passed on to descendants, as was the case with Henry and Victor. We can but speculate about how proud the parents would have been about Philip's overseas sporting achievements, Clive's medical studies in London and Ralph's mining engineer activities in South Africa. Certainly in letters from the parents to Henry and Victor there are periodic comments about their other sons' doings. Letters from Henry and Victor to their parents also mention Philip, Clive and Ralph, but usually only in passing and not in great detail. This seems to have been a common thread: these men appear not to have communicated a great deal with each other and about each other, seemingly a family trait

As we have seen, Simpson Newland's third and last book, *Memoirs of Simpson Newland CMG,* published in 1926, says surprisingly little about his children – and he makes the point for his not doing so eloquently: 'Of my family life I will say but little, for I am not one of those who believe in laying bare the intimacies of home'. In his book, quoted earlier (page xi), Simpson explains the qualities he had hoped to instil in his sons and which he considered so important, these including self-reliance, capability and resilience, along with taking individual responsibility. These were the qualities he believed would 'make men' of his sons, and given what they achieved, it appears that he was successful, although the evidence for Clive and Ralph may be less conclusive. I certainly recall my father displaying similar characteristics, albeit in a different context. He seemed to want my sisters and me to emulate similar values as well as we could in our various ways in the latter part of the twentieth century.

In his 2003 book *Mountains of the Mind,*[11] Robert McFarlane makes the following comment about John Ruskin's views on character and bravery:

> Ruskin's equation of effeminacy with lifelessness, weakness and error is a sour reminder of how tightly braided ideas of bravery were with ideas of masculinity at that time (1863). But his point is also distinctly Victorian in the belief that overcoming danger made one a 'better person'. Nietzsche, a more famous metaphysician of fear than Ruskin, would later put it more punchily; what doesn't kill you makes you stronger. Risk taking – scaring yourself – was, provided you survived, a potent means of self-improvement. And self-improvement was to later Victorians a powerfully attractive ideal (p. 86).

To my mind, this quotation from McFarlane's book is relevant to the idea of the 'making' of these sons as men in their parents' eyes. In addition to, or quite likely as a key part of Simpson and Jane's aspirations, all five sons married women of substance in the growing colony of South Australia. The backgrounds, stories and circumstances of these women are interesting in themselves, given their respective family origins. Although little detail will be given about them in this book, their role in the lives of the five sons, as wives and as mothers to their children, and their influence on their husbands and children where known, is mentioned where relevant.

The five Newland sons with their parents. Standing, from left: Ralph, Henry and Philip; seated:, Victor, Simpson (father), Jane (mother) and Clive, c. 1900.

As I explained earlier, I have met only one of these five sons. When I was a small child in the mid-1950s, Henry Simpson, Sir Henry, or Uncle Hal as we called him, was still very much alive, and living with his wife Ellen (my Great Aunt Nell) in the suburb of Walkerville in northern Adelaide. I remember him as a smallish, although somewhat intimidating, man, quite lively for his age (then in his late eighties) and quite deaf.

Stories about him as a 'character about town' abounded. His driving habits on North Terrace, a major street in Adelaide, were notorious: people were careful to keep out of the way when he was behind the steering wheel of his Austin A40 car, registered as SA 99, if they valued their lives. My second cousins Henry and John tell me that his wife, their grandmother, had an Austin A30 registered as SA 77. They knew Uncle Hal much better than did I and describe him as a man of iron will who did not suffer fools. Notwithstanding these characteristics and his remarkable achievements, he didn't display any sense of self-importance and as a grandfather was, according to them, kindly and generous. As with most of his brothers, Henry senior was physically not a large man, which is not surprising, given that his own father was so small at 160 cm (5 feet or thereabouts).

There is too little information about Philip compared with his elder brother to say more than has been said in the chapter devoted to him (Chapter 6), which reveals that he was an exceptional sportsman and a man of charm, whose life from his late twenties until his death in his early forties was, unfortunately, a fairly miserable one.

Victor Marra, or Mick as he was known, was also still alive in my early life, although regretfully I never met him. I can recall my mother speaking affectionately about him as 'Uncle Mick'. His granddaughter Leonie Matheson, along with her mother (Victor's younger daughter), lived with him for much of Leonie's early life, as her father had died when she was four years old. She was very fond of him and describes him as a soldier and adventurer, among many other things.[12]

The stories in the subsequent chapters about Clive and Ralph reflect the lack of information about them, particularly compared with Henry and Victor, although the information I have collated has been valuable in shedding some light on these two men, one of whom (Ralph) was described by his youngest son Malcolm – my uncle – as 'a shadowy figure'. There is no evidence to confirm the accuracy of this description; it is more likely to have been a reflection of the unfortunate manner by which Ralph's motherless children were raised.

It is clear that Henry and Victor were of great comfort to Simpson and presumably Jane, with whom they had a close relationship, both when they were younger men, as their letters show, and in their parents' old age. The premature deaths of the other three sons is most likely to have reinforced this relationship.

The truncated lives of Philip, Clive and Ralph, along with a lack of a records, specifically letters, means that I have principally relied on Henry's and Victor's letters and other records such as press cuttings and family photographs in my attempt to piece together a description of each of the sons. It has become clear from the letter record that Clive was a favourite of his father's, but the reasons for this are not known.

A chapter for each of the sons follows, and obviously some chapters will be much more comprehensive than others. I have sought and received information from those cousins of mine who are direct descendants of the respective sons and for that I am most grateful. I have added my own insights and extra information where appropriate and relevant, gleaned from my own research.

5

Henry Simpson Newland

BORN 24 NOVEMBER 1873, DIED 13 NOVEMBER 1969

The first of the sons, Henry Simpson Newland, was born in Kensington, Adelaide, in 1873. His father Simpson was still very much involved in the pastoral industry, managing three station properties on the Darling River in New South Wales (Marra, Warlo and Buckanbe) and another on the NSW–Queensland border adjoining the Paroo River (Talyealye). While there is no known record to explain why Simpson chose this location in another state, it seems that he was invited to join a partnership that involved his future brother-in-law. The conditions must have been attractive as well, including having a reasonably secure supply of water from the Darling River, so important for a successful pastoral enterprise.

A large portion of the first three years of Henry's life was spent at Marra. These were times when transport for individuals was largely by horseback, with horses and coach or paddle steamer used for groups of people. Journeys by means of these forms of transport often covered large distances, usually under what today would be regarded as uncomfortable and inconvenient conditions. Among the family records is an account of a horse and coach trip to Sydney taken by Henry and his parents when he was about two years old. This journey ended up taking several days due to bad weather, having to wait for other passengers, the threat of bushrangers and the need to change horses periodically. The trip was also affected by coach drivers who were not always sober.

Children are influenced by experiences early in life and it can be quite reasonably assumed that the young Henry absorbed much of what was around him. He would have been close to his mother and also would have seen his father displaying the sorts of manly characteristics described earlier. Notwithstanding the difficulties Jane is likely to have experienced in such isolation, Henry must have been great comfort to his mother during the regular absences of his father out on the pastoral runs. This situation also says something about Jane's strength of character, her resilience and her capacity to cope and deal with living in such harsh and isolated circumstances. After all, she was not even twenty-five years old and the mother of a child. It is clear from Simpson's letters at that time that she did have other support, but she lived under difficult and risky conditions in a house alongside the Darling River, a river that had already claimed the lives of two of Simpson's nieces. In 1862, Jane and Henrietta Field, aged twelve and four, had drowned at the same time in tragic circumstances. There were misunderstandings involving both European and Aboriginal people, the latter having certain strong cultural beliefs about that part of the river.

In addition to maternal influence, Henry's early formal education was provided by a governess, probably at what became the family mansion Undelcarra in Burnside, Adelaide, to which the family moved when he was a little over three years old. He (and his brothers) went initially to Queen's School in North Adelaide and then on to St Peter's College in Hackney, Adelaide, for much of their education. Henry chose to train as a doctor after he had finished secondary schooling. Although Henry's performance as a student was initially not particularly outstanding, it improved markedly by the time he was in his fifth year. It appears that management problems at the Adelaide Hospital led him to decide in 1897 to undertake postgraduate studies in London. However, these problems were likely not the sole reason for his decision: England was regarded as 'home' for many people of this era and Henry appears to be no exception.

A biography of Henry already exists – written by Dr J. Escourt-Hughes[13] – and I acknowledge that work and have drawn some information from it, but I do not intend to repeat what has already been recorded about Henry's life of ninety-six years. Published in 1972 by the South Australian Fellows of the Royal Australasian College of Surgeons and now out of print, it has a strong medical emphasis. As a man of medicine, Henry's achievements at that time are bordering on legendary. I am grateful to my second cousin (also Dr Henry Simpson Newland) for pointing out some of those achievements. For example, Henry senior told him that 'to be a good surgeon, you need the heart of a lion and hands of a lady'. He is said to have operated on every organ in the body and his war record is testament to the extent of his experience and skill.

Henry's skill was not confined to surgery: in 1962 he established the Australian Medical Association, modelled on the British Medical Association (BMA), for which he received the BMA's highest honour. In 1946, prior to a Commonwealth referendum, he met with the federal Leader of the Opposition, Robert Menzies, and persuaded him that doctors and dentists should be able to charge an additional amount above any fee payment by government (the gap fee), an amount that the doctor believed represented his or her skill level.

Henry Simpson Newland at graduation from Medical School, 1897.

The biography's foreword, written by Sir Edward Morgan, refers to the sorts of attributes that this book on the making of men, but written forty-five years later, attempts to elucidate:

> I believe Sir Henry Simpson Newland owed his great success in life to four things, all of them of iron. They were: his constitution; his will-power; his determination to carry through to the best of his ability anything which he undertook; finally, his sense of what was right and wrong.

It is reasonable to suggest that Henry can thank his parents, his circumstances, his education and indeed himself for the possession of these four characteristics. It is likely that he acted as something of a role model for his four younger brothers. They could scarcely not notice such attributes in their older brother.

In 1889, at the age of fifteen and while still at St Peter's College, he and his family travelled to England via France. Thus early in his life he was exposed to what would have been perceived in the day as the 'glories of the British Empire' and which may have become something of an influence in his later life on the battlefields of Egypt, Gallipoli, France and at hospitals in Lemnos and later in London, as some of the letters reproduced later suggest.

Henry completed his secondary schooling when the Newland family returned to Adelaide, and in 1892 went on to Medical School at the University of Adelaide. The Escourt-Hughes biography notes that he was equal top in his graduation year. Then followed several years of postgraduate study and work in both London and in Adelaide as a partner to a Dr Robert Marten. During this time, Henry developed various surgical techniques that were to hold him in good stead for the sorts of conditions that would prevail during the First World War. A trip to England in 1907 furthered his already extensive medical experience. In 1908, be became Honorary Surgeon at the Adelaide Children's Hospital. He married Ellen Mary Lindon on 14 July 1910. They had three children before the outbreak of war in 1914.

Henry enlisted voluntarily in November of that year, something that he regarded as a matter of course for any male in his situation and it said that he was the first married man from South Australia to enlist. His parents of course would not have expected anything less. Interestingly, the Escourt-Hughes biography records that, with the exception of the commanding officer Lieutenant-Colonel H.W. Bryant, all of the medical officers of the unit at that time were from South Australia. They were Majors H.A. Powell, A. Watson, T.G. Wilson and H.S. Newland and Captains F.N. LeMessurier, J.S. Verco and J. Corbin.

In an attempt to build on this largely unrecorded yet remarkable stage of Henry's life as a younger man, my sisters and I have researched letters from Henry to his parents held in the State Library during the time of the First World War and also those to his brothers. To my knowledge these letters have not been seriously studied before. I have tried to discover more about what drove this essentially private and self-effacing man to achieve so much. These letters are numerous and I may well have missed some important facts and reflections.

Henry's four characteristics – identified in the foreword to Escourt-Hughes's book – feature strongly in the excerpts of the letters used in this account. The letters were sent mainly to his parents and occasionally to one of his brothers. The 'iron' characteristics of constitution, willpower, determination and a sense of right and wrong are evident in so much in what Henry did during his life, and his assessment of what he was doing. Despite the horrors and senseless slaughter of war, Henry worked unremittingly to save the lives of wounded men in what are now recognised as the worst theatres of the First World War – Gallipoli, Egypt and France.

The fact that Henry 'saw it through' and lived to develop a successful surgical practice on his return to South Australia says more about his resilience and strength than can be done justice in any book. From what I've uncovered about the circumstances that he faced during the First World War, it seems remarkable to me that he survived so well and went on to a stellar life and career. He battled on year after year and almost seemed to thrive on what many others were unable to cope with.

On the outbreak of the First World War, Henry went first to Egypt, subsequently travelling, in 1915, to what he called Anzac as a 'repair' surgeon. From there, he went to Ypres and from there, in 1916, to the Somme. By this time he was a lieutenant-colonel, although the administrative work associated with the military establishment appears not to have suited him. In Egypt in July 1915, as commanding officer of a new medical unit, Henry was pleased to receive new equipment, as much had been lost during the earlier withdrawal from Anzac Cove. His letters indicate that he expected to go to Anzac 'at last' from Lemnos, although puzzlingly he did not expect much surgical work there. Earlier, on 22 February of that year, he wrote to his parents indicating that his sense of duty was affronted by the casual nature of the Australian troops he observed. This opinion was to change markedly in a year's time:

> One does not feel at all proud of the Australian troops … they have been too lax and the consequence is the discipline is very poor – the New Zealanders who have more Imperial officers seem to me to have a much better sense of responsibility. The Light Horse seem to be a much better class of men.

While his younger brother Philip has his own story, Henry, despite the heavy burden of medical practice on the battlefield, still found time to be concerned about his unwell younger brother. In 1915 he hopes at this time 'that things are as well as they can be with Phil and that he is not getting any bad turns'. He also refers on 24 June 1915 to many sick and wounded soldiers coming to a medical aid station 'at the Peninsula' from Cape Hellas and Gaba Tefel, the location of the Australians in Palestine. Interestingly, in this letter he also shows uncharacteristic bitterness in saying:

> Many of us are feeling very sore that those who hung back at first, like Cudmore and de Crespigny, should have been rewarded by being given more important posts [in Adelaide] than those which were awarded to those who volunteered promptly. Anyway, I will always be proud to know that I was the first married man with a family in Adelaide to volunteer.

Despite his appalling experiences at Anzac Cove, Henry was prepared to give the Turks credit where it was due, for example, manoeuvring 8-inch guns across the desert. However, he seemed to think that the Turks would have limited capacity to achieve much after February 1916. Henry's clear preference was working where his surgical skills would be of most use, and in December 1915 in Anzac Cove he reports Turkish shells landing around the hospital, killing and wounding patients. He notes at the time that the Turks really should not be blamed for 'stray shells' landing in the hospital compound, since it was, according to him, located near stores of ammunition. He also noted, in the six weeks he was at Anzac, that he and his team 'were under fire all the time and that we never once slept under shelter; I mean shelter from shells'. The hospital was to have been moved to the other side of the peninsula, where it would have been safe from Turkish guns. Henry appears to have been working in this hospital of 1000 beds and was in charge of 500 beds.

Notwithstanding his initial impression of the Australian troops, he later expressed admiration for the Australian spirit:

> it takes a lot to damp the spirits of an Australian. I used to have rather a dislike to the free and easy and independent bearing of the young Australian, but I prefer it to the humble attitude of the British Tommy and it makes him a perfect dare devil when it comes to fighting.

For part of 1916, Henry was stationed at a Belgian hospital, which enabled him to use and further develop new methods of dressing wounds. During this time, his letters refer to the 'infernal Germans' being difficult to beat and that fighting will have to continue until the Allies are 'able to dictate terms'. From a battlefield clearing station in September 1916 he wrote of his admiration for an airman who was hit by a bullet in the brain and who, 'after falling 1000 feet, righted his aeroplane and then landed beside the hospital he wanted to enter'. Another airman, after being hit by a German high explosive: 'fell 2000 feet. His engine stopped when he was hit but he was able to land behind our lines with his machine quite undamaged'.

Henry returned to England in late 1916, and from the Australian General Hospital in Brighton, he wrote to his mother on 22 January 1917: 'I saw over 200 armless or legless soldiers a week ago. They are all fitted with excellent artificial limbs before they are sent to Australia'.

Remarkably, given what he had already been through, in February 1917 Henry travelled to Flanders. He wrote to his mother on 20 February 1917 to tell her of his plans:

> I am going to the Clearing Station commanded by John Corbin which I believe is on the Somme near Alberl. I will be Surgical Specialist and entirely responsible for surgery. I think it very probable that I shall get good work and plenty of it.

He arrived there on 5 March 1917 as the most senior Australian surgeon, noting on 18 March 1917 that 'the work is strenuous but vastly interesting'. At the end of that month Henry walked over a battleground taken by Britain some months earlier, describing it as a place of utter devastation and 'a melancholy sight'. He was searching for a grave of a cousin of his wife Nell, which he finally found and 'spent some time making the grave tidy, although it was rather gruesome having to be done under fire and carried out in a perfunctory manner'.

On 28 April 1917 he wrote to his parents that fighting was fierce and that he had had: 'a tremendous lot of big operative work, often going all night. I have had 80 big operations in 3 weeks, 22 of them being abdominal cases'. Despite this workload, he wrote on 9 May that 'it was bad luck getting influenza after 2 years of continuous work which pulled me down a little'.

In that year, Henry was awarded the Distinguished Services Order (DSO), with personal congratulations from General Birdwood. When he wrote to his mother on 14 April, he commented: 'For myself, honours are nothing as long as I can return to Australia with my self-respect, but for your and the Pater's and Nell's sake'.

Henry's parents were concerned that he might not return to Australia, as he clearly was something of an Anglophile, having spent some time there after completing his medical studies in Adelaide. On 13 May 1917 he wrote from Flanders reassuringly to his father:

> Mr Lindon [his father-in-law] writes that you and the Mater are much upset at the suggestion of my remaining in England to practise. I have not the slightest intention of doing so unless something superlatively good is offered ... I consider my chances of ultimate success in Adelaide are as brilliant as I would wish them to be.

Nine days later he tells his mother that 'shells and grenades so often produce fearful, complicating wounds of the head, chest or limbs'.

Henry's devotion to his wife Ellen (or Nell), whom he married in mid-1910 and who visited him in England during the war, was poignantly shown in another letter to his parents. Even though he was in one of the worst locations of the First World War in terms of the sheer human carnage – Flanders – he wrote on 18 July 1917:

> Nell has at long last left for Australia via Canada. I myself have been most wretchedly depressed by her departure and I cannot say how fervently I long for the end of this war. This separation from Nell almost breaks down one's resolution at times.

He continued along these lines when writing to his mother twelve days later, his letter also revealing something of his eternal determination to see things through:

> I am sure she will be very miserable for some time. Very nearly half our married life has now been spent apart and we are both utterly fed up with it. However, we are both just as determined as ever to give of our best and when the end of the war comes, neither of us will, I hope, have anything to reproach ourselves with.

He also expressed concern that his children may forget that they have a father.

Henry's descriptions of the horrors of the Western Front are many and include the following examples. On 5 August 1917, he wrote to his father:

> We had 16 high explosive shells which burst near us and fragments of two of them rattled against the hut in which we were operating. It is not pleasant to hear the shells screaming overhead and wondering whether the next is going to land on the hut.

Later that month he wrote:

> The fighting has been terribly fierce in these parts. At times the work has been overwhelming and during the last ten days I have only been to bed one night in two. Last night I operated all night in 4 abdominal cases and 2 head cases.

Towards the end of the year Henry recounted:

> Though hard fighting continues and the guns have been thundering away for the last 36 hours, we have had quite a slack time … I am feeling much stronger and fitter and many marvel at the long hours I am able to work … It is extraordinary how one can keep operating all the time and not get tired.

On 1 October 1917, he once again displayed his resilience and tenacity, despite appalling conditions, writing to his parents:

> Nearly 1500 operations have been done in the last month. I hope I shall be left in France for a couple of months longer to continue this work … I am kept very busy doing chest surgery. It is intensely interesting work but it is very exacting as it is hard to cope with so many cases in a week. If one ever dreamed of operating on the chest and lungs at the start of the war [sic].

> From three patients I removed large fragments of shell which were embedded in the lung. By operating early one is able to prevent the chest from getting septic … I am glad to say that I am not much disturbed at night by them [aeroplanes]. Some men are acutely miserable and sleepless whenever a hostile plane is overhead. But one has to get used to it or one would have many sleepless nights.

A few days later, he once again describes the difficult conditions under they work:

> The weather is miserably cold and wet and as a shell blew most of our oil stoves and other heating material to pieces a week ago, the warmest place is [illegible text] I have had a rather good run of additional cases lately: 24 out of the last 29 penetrating wounds … have recovered.

A fortnight later, he once again described the harrowing working conditions:

> We have 6 operating tables going all day and other operating we can relieve … is at night. I see all the worst and dreadful cases … I am keeping fit, though a good many of our officers have been sick lately.

Notwithstanding Henry's obvious ability to cope, he showed his capacity for empathy, also demonstrating that he recognised what some of his patients were experiencing, writing to his father on 28 October 1917:

> I have just had 2 very heavy days operating. The weather is so deplorable that a man would suffer greatly from shock, from cold and lying out before the stretcher-bearers find him in the shell craters. How some of them ever survive I don't know.

On this same day, Henry advised that he had received notice that he may be called to a military hospital specialising in jaw wounds, in Kent, England. Despite what he had been through, he expressed a desire to remain in France to write up the work he had been doing. He continued to worry about the effect of his absence on his wife and children, but, as he said in his letter in July 1917 to his parents:

> when one sees the man in the trenches sticking it out and giving only too often his life, one feels … to go back. The man who is killed has one advantage; he has no knowledge of the sacrifice he is making. I make my sacrifice of home and money willingly enough but nothing can ever give me back the years I have missed with Nell and the kiddies. And it is very hard on you both too …

Henry returned to England in December 1917 and remained at the Queen's Hospital in Kent until his eventual recall to Australia via London. He wrote to his father from Kent: 'for Australian soldiers I am honourbound to return to Australia to do all I can for those who have given of their best'.

Henry's 1918 letters refer to the Australian campaign in Villers Bretonneux and the saving of Amiens and also what he described as 'the very large sum' his father had sent to London to help him start his practice again. In a letter dated 18 February 1918 he wrote:

> for three nights in succession the Hun has now raided London and he is making merry as I write. The people get absurdly terrified and flock very unnecessarily into all the underground railway tubes … When I reached London an air raid was in progress and I found the tube stations a mass of stinking humanity. Personally

> I think a great deal too much is made of the raids which do very little real harm.

The dangerous conditions he had faced in France probably prompted this assessment of the London situation.

Henry showed that he was not entirely selfless by writing the following to his father from London, showing a degree of uncharacteristic and possibly naive bitterness. Given what he had been through, perhaps he could be forgiven for writing:

> There is no doubt that the people of Australia take no pride in sacrifice and do not realise what a German victory would mean. I wish a German raider could get loose and bomb Sydney and Melbourne. It would do all the good in the world.

Later on in this letter, Henry describes the importance of the work he is doing:

> surgery of the only part of the human body which is capable of showing expression demands great skill, meticulous care and something of the artist. It does not matter much what a scar on the belly looks like, but it does very much matter on the face – a great deal of it is pioneer work and therefore all the more absorbing.

In 1919, he was awarded a Commander of the British Empire (CBE).

Henry returned to Adelaide in 1919, by which time he was in his mid-forties. He established a successful surgical practice and also held various teaching posts at the University of Adelaide Medical School. (Further details of this aspect of his life are spelled out in Estcourt-Hughes's biography.) As with his brothers, he was keenly interested in sport, particularly rowing, cricket, football and tennis. He was a keen supporter of the Norwood Football Club, undoubtedly because of his younger brother Philip's involvement, details of which are given in Chapter 6. He started playing bowls when he turned ninety. For many years he was Patron of the Adelaide University Boat Club, which was established in 1881. He had been a member of a crew of eight who won the Australian Universities boat race in 1886.

He was made a KCMG (Order of St Michael and St George) in 1928 and became involved in voluntary activities well beyond medicine. Among these was the Wyatt Benevolent Trust, which his father before him, as a friend of Dr William Wyatt, had been instrumental in establishing, in 1881. Henry was chairman of the Trust Board for thirty years! Perhaps he hoped to eclipse his father's service!

Henry was also involved in various other entities, mainly associated with medicine and wellbeing and often as an office holder. As flagged earlier, he founded the Royal Australian College of Surgeons and received gold medals for his service to the Australian Medical Association, amongst others.

Despite considering a working life in England around the start of the First World War, Henry remained staunchly wedded to and supportive of South Australia once he had returned from England. He was respected by all, although probably also feared by some, as he was not one to suffer fools.

His grandson Henry, who is my second cousin, is the only person alive who knew his grandfather well and he has passed on to me several pieces of information. Some of these are historically important, others amusing and others less so. One of the former related to the removal of Colonel Light's statue from Light Square in Adelaide to Montefiore Hill. This move was attributed to Henry, who considered the new location more suitable, even though it meant re-routing the Montefiore Hill road.

Among the amusing anecdotes one relates to the way by which Henry drove his car, the long-suffering Austin A40. According to my cousin Henry, as Henry senior's deafness advanced, the only way he could tell whether his car was running was by 'revving' it until he could feel it vibrating under him. He was not interested in road rules and was something of a terror between the Royal Adelaide Hospital and the Adelaide Club, both on North Terrace. He is reputed to have driven from Victor Harbor to Adelaide in first gear because for some reason he did not or could not change gears. He lived in Belt St, Walkerville, a suburb close to the centre of Adelaide, where in his later years, he grew fruit trees. He was known to flood his downhill neighbour when he forgot to turn off taps.

Henry senior used his deafness to ignore those with whom he did not want to converse, including his wife. She endured his idiosyncratic ways, which included him staying overnight at the Adelaide Club when the mood took him rather than going home. Notwithstanding Henry senior's peculiarities and his tendency to be stern and gruff, Henry junior remembers him as a gentleman with a real sense of humour. As with his father and grandfather, Henry was keen on trips to Victor Harbor, where, as a founding member, he had given land to the Victor Harbor Golf Club. Henry junior recalls going to the golf course with his grandfather on a mission to control the burgeoning wild rabbit numbers with mustard gas and nearly asphyxiating themselves!

Henry senior loved fishing and Henry junior remembers well in the 1950s the wooden boat he kept at Colombury, the house he had built at Victor Harbor, opposite Granite Island. This boat was dragged along a rail track to the water by horse. Henry junior also remembers an aloof man who liked a good time and yet who combined his aloofness with generosity and humility. Henry senior clearly was proud of his achievements and grateful for his heritage, which he was not backward in using to his advantage.

He died in November 1969 at the age of ninety-six. Estcourt-Hughes, at the end of his biography, gives his assessment of Simpson and Jane's eldest son:

> I have known clearness of judgement, largeness of fancy, strength of reason, graceful elocution, a courage for the wars, fear of the laws, grandeur of bearing – all eminently in one man.

While this quotation had been used previously to describe a seventeenth-century statesman (Sidney Godolpin), it is praise indeed in the early 1970s for the first of these remarkable sons of Simpson and Jane.

6

Philip Mesmer Newland

BORN 2 FEBRUARY 1875, DIED 11 AUGUST 1916

Simpson and Jane's second son Philip was born in February 1875 in New South Wales, possibly at Junee or at Marra station. As the dates above indicate, his was a relatively short life, of just over forty years. One can but speculate on what he might have achieved had he lived healthily for another twenty or thirty years. Philip's foreshortened life may well have resulted from a sporting accident. Whatever the cause, there is little doubt that the last ten years of his life were difficult, as this chapter recounts.

Like his brothers, Phil, as he quickly came to be known, went to Queen's School and then on to St Peter's College. He then studied law at the University of Adelaide. He was articled to the Chief Justice (Hon G.J. Murray) and was admitted to the bar in 1899. Soon after, Phil went into partnership with the Hon. F.W. Young, previously agent-general for South Australia in London. This partnership lasted until 1911, when H.T. Ward joined the firm. Phil was a first-class athlete, excelling in cricket, football and lacrosse. He was regarded as one of the country's best interstate lacrosse players, playing until he was nearly thirty.

Unfortunately, as far as is known by the Newland family, no letters written by Phil have survived. His immediate younger brother Victor wrote to him both from the ship on his voyage to Africa and also while Victor was in Africa. Father Simpson's letters to his first son and Phil's elder brother Henry say something of Phil's sporting abilities and his capacity to charm the opposite sex, as a letter dated 12 July 1897 from Undelcarra demonstrates:

> I have just had a week in Melbourne where I went to see about publishing my new book & other business combined with a desire to witness the La crosse matches. The team stayed at the Grand whence I followed two days later. I enjoyed the trip much, one of the matches especially, this against the MCC. It was a beautiful afternoon & Phil was the hero of the occasion, & made 6 goals out of 7. There was great excitement & much cheering. I met my old friend Geo Rolfe, dined with him, his wife & three step daughters on Sunday, all grown up nice girls – & arranged for them to attend the game on the Tuesday. I introduced them to Phil & they got very excited over his success. It was the first time they had had ever seen La-crosse played & they were delighted with it. The Sydney men were duffers far below the worst Melbourne team that played. I was glad to see our Varsity men more than held their own.

Philip's younger brothers Clive and Ralph, the youngest of Simpson's sons, were also lacrosse players and played in teams with him. The photograph opposite was taken in 1898 in the portico of the Mitchell Building at the University of Adelaide and shows Philip in the middle row, second from the left, with Clive seated on the left front.

The family has a similar photo taken over two years later which shows Philip and Ralph, not Clive.

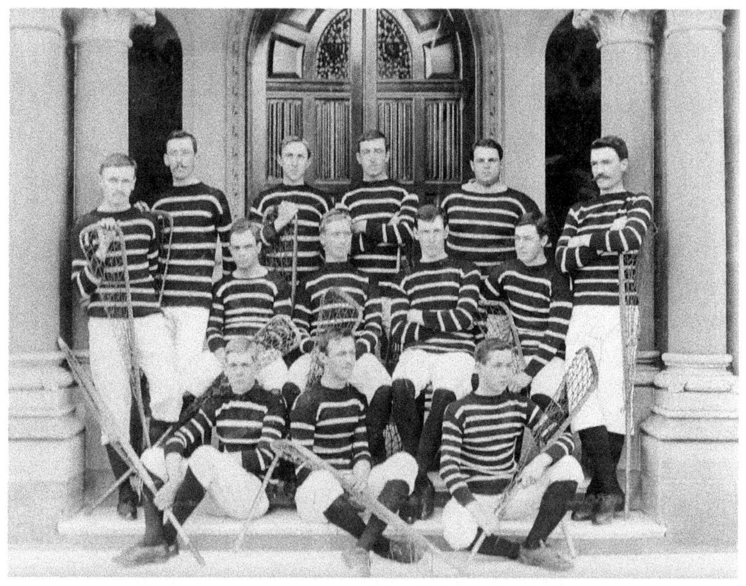

University A team SA Lacrosse Association 1901. Philip, the captain, is second from the left in the middle row, and Clive, first from the left, front row.

Philip also played league football for the Norwood Football Club and captained the winning 1904 premiership team. The team was thirty-five points down at three-quarter time and went on to win, no mean feat at this level of the game.

As noted earlier, as well as an excellent athlete, Philip was often described as a charming man. He married Josephine Mary Ferguson on 20 February 1905, just after his thirtieth birthday. The Fergusons were near neighbours at Undelcarra, residing in the large house, Chiverton, which is now part of St Peter's Girls School, in the Adelaide foothills. The wedding reception was held at Chiverton, with the wedding cake decorated with white-icing cricket bats, balls and cricketing jerseys, in acknowledgement of Philip's sporting prowess.

Photographs in the family's possession show that the Newland boys often visited Chiverton for tennis parties and, I suspect, for socialising with the Ferguson children. There were four Ferguson children, two boys and two girls, born over a six-year period from 1906 to 1912.

Philip made his debut in first-class Test cricket in 1899, playing until 1906. In 1905 he was selected to play for Australia against England in Joe Darling's Australian Eleven as second wicket keeper. Other well-known players were Victor Trumper, Clem Hill and Monty Noble. Direct descendants of Philip's, my cousins Phill Newland and his sister Karen Aird, have provided some information about their grandfather and his undoubted sporting abilities.

One piece of information comes from the Queensland Cricket Association. An article from 'Cricket, a Weekly Record of the Game', dated 20 April 1905, describes two new Australian cricketers, of which Philip Newland was one. The article points out that a second wicket keeper has few chances to distinguish himself during a tour of England, but emphasises the critical role a wicket keeper plays in the game, meaning therefore a wicket keeper understudy should not be ignored. The article notes:

> There are many good judges in Australia who think that Carter is a better wicket-keeper than Newland but he happens to be a New South Wales man and as Kelly is the first wicket-keeper for the State, his understudy has few chances of coming to the front. Newland on the other hand is the chief wicket-keeper for South Australia, and has therefore had opportunities of showing his skill in the great matches. Newland is not 'showy' in his methods and like nearly all wicket-keepers who have become famous, he contrives to make his work look ridiculously easy and

> simple. His strongest point seems to be consistency; he does not do wonderful things on one day, only to miss many chances on the next and naturally such a man is to be preferred to others who in a particular match may appear brilliant performers. As a batsman Newland is not attractive to watch; he is one of the stubborn school who are more popular with their own teams than with spectators. But on several occasions he has shown his ability to keep his end safe while a more brilliant player has been making runs … During the recent Australian season he kept up his form as a wicket-keeper and cricketers were prepared to some extent to find his name on the list of Australians who were to go to England. There seems no doubt at all that he is a most capable wicket-keeper and as he is young, it is more than likely that in coming years he will be the successor to Kelly.

Philip played ten first-class matches while in the United Kingdom. Unfortunately, he was injured while practising cricket on the ship voyage to London, having been hit on the head by a cricket ball when the ship rolled, resulting in an eye injury. His playing performance while in England was not outstanding and it is quite likely that his playing had been affected by this injury. It is not unreasonable to assume that this injury cut short his long-term sporting opportunities, effectively ending his first-class cricket aspirations, even though he continued to play some sport for several years after this particular incident. The incident appears to have contributed to his life being miserable and may have led to his early death from a brain tumour.

When Philip returned to South Australia, he completed his legal studies at the University of Adelaide. He either became a partner, or he was a partner before he left for England, in the legal firm of Young, Newland and Ward, solicitors of Adelaide. Lack of

Philip Mesmer Newland c. 1905.

definitive information means that the timing of these events is unclear.

A second article about lacrosse (the date is unknown but it appears to be early in the twentieth century) makes some interesting observations about Philip, who was the captain of the South Australian team. He was regarded as:

> the champion 'home' of Australia and the tussles between him and Sutherland, the Victorian – and possibly Australian – champion defence player, were worth going a long way to see. Both have every reason to be satisfied with their performances.

It is clear from the few letters the Newland family has in its possession that Philip as a younger man was well regarded by his brothers, especially by Victor, to whom he was closest in age. Victor, in a letter to his parents from South Africa, had some interesting comments about Philip's love life:

> By the by Phil is not attached to Jo [one of the Ferguson girls who Phil eventually married], it is to Miss Bessie, who unluckily for him, does not reciprocate. It is this I think that makes Phil a bit down – it is very silly of him to be so despondent.

Victor's letters refer to Philip on several occasions, including a couple written directly to him. The one reproduced below, dated 31 January 1900, written when Victor was on the ship heading to the Boer War, offers a good example of two impulsive and reckless young men writing to each other. It has a 'macho' flavour, referring among other things to daring deeds, money, women and drinking, all issues that may well have resonated with them both. It certainly says a lot about Victor and his eternal optimism, which emerges clearly in Chapter 7.

> SS 'Surrey'
> 31/1/1900
> My dear Phil
>
> I have written a long letter to the 'Register' and you will there get all the news of our trip. I have had a grand time – not been a bit sick – had jolly fine meals and comfortable hammock with other luxuries such as a salt shower and sundry cases of fruit. It has been most laughable to see the other chaps sprawling about. Horses on board ship are an abomination. I have been appointed (temporarily) Assistant Orderly Clerk and have nothing to do but write orders and attend such drills as I think fit – it is good fun

for a spell whilst the others are sick, and so incapable mates, but I am going to chuck it up soon, as I am getting too fat and soft. I was boxing today barefooted and caught my sole on a rivet – result a decidedly sore foot and a limp. Yesterday I went down into the refrigerator and lumped up carcasses – the last side of beef nearly killed me: it slipped from the slings and touched me on shoulder and legs – another 3' and there would have been no fighting in the Transvaal for me.

We passed Albany this afternoon and have since been steering either dead for land or away from it: it seems queer, but I suppose the Officers know what they are doing. Most of our men are turning up trumps and I have never been sorry since I joined the contingent: I am sure it will be a great experience. The farewells on the wharf were very sad: poor little Marion and Gracie Way seemed very cut up at Jim's departure. Give them my love and say that he is losing the pathetic look in his blue eyes that mal der mer gave them and is plucking up grandly: it is great to have such good chums with us.

I have written Miss Little that you would let her have a photo of me – please see that she gets it. We get to Fremantle tomorrow night; afterwards you will see where we land and will address letters accordingly. Remember me to all friends, particularly Fenner and tell him his knife has been most useful, particularly the corkscrew. No doubt you have fixed up all finance etc. with Elders: if you can get any letters of introduction for me, please do so – send them on to Seawrights to be left till called for. Best wishes to you both.

From your affec. brother
VM Newland

In another letter to Phil a couple of months later, Victor recounts his exploits in an understated way, these apparently the reason for his being awarded the DCM (Distinguished Conduct Medal). As with so many of Victor's letters, it is full of action and drama:

> In train 29/3/1900
>
> My dear Phil,
>
> We returned the day before yesterday from the relief of Prieska having covered since we left De Aar some 250 miles on horseback. I have written to the paper how we rode into Prieska so will say nothing more about it. I am awfully pleased that having been the first of our crowd to get across the Orange River. The next day after our swim I lost all my money and valuables sliding along the punt cable to rig up a cradle so that the Officers might land dry footed. I have been lucky in having a splendid horse, though he is a brute to ride sometimes, kicking like the devil – one day he kicked so high that he was hitting me in the back with his rump and finally landed me with a sprained thumb – the Prieska ride has taken the vice out of him all right now. During our ride back we had about 7" of rain: we were without tents and you can imagine the bliss of being wet to the skin, puddling through mud and riding in soaked saddles – following the rain we had heavy dews, so that our health has been fairly tested – thank goodness I am in great fettle. We are now on our way to Bloemfontein to the very seat of the war, where Kitchener and Roberts are and are bound to see a good deal of the game. Kitchener was with us on our ride to Prieska and spoke a few words to my troop – I have never seen a man with so absolutely an imperturbable face. Our army then was 2500 men and we had with us 150 transport wagons, so that Lord Robert's 40 to 50,000 men must have a huge train with them. Everyone thinks so much of Australians that we are awfully proud of ourselves – only hope we will do well now

> that we are on our way to Pretoria. I have not yet fired a shot, though we have seen scattered flying Boers in the distance and two of our dispatch carriers were fired on. Francie Bell is with us and in my four – he is very good fun. Remember me to the Fergies and with love to you and Ralph.
>
> I am your affec brother
>
> VM Newland

Both Henry and Clive were probably away working and studying in England at the time of this letter. Ralph would have been living at Undelcarra.

As can be seen from the beginning of this chapter, Philip was no ordinary person. Family photographs show him as a bold man and one wonders what he might have made of brother Victor's adventures in Africa while he was in South Australia and elsewhere playing a great deal of sport, challenging his body and mind in a different way.

Some years after he was married, Philip and his family moved to Balaklava in the lower north of South Australia, probably around 1910, when he was in his mid-thirties; here he managed a branch of his legal firm. Although it is not entirely clear, it seems that the move may have been prompted by his failing health. In addition to or as a result of the sporting injury he had received, Philip had developed a tumour on the brain. In a letter from their father, dated 31 December 1914, to eldest son Henry, who was serving as a medical officer during the First World War, Simpson reports as follows:

> Phil has been to the hospital for over a fortnight & gone home with another nurse who seems a success. On the whole, Phil

appears to be much the same as when you left tho' somewhat disappointed at our thus far none success [*sic*].

Excerpts from a letter from Henry, dated 15 July 1915 and written from England to their mother, give some idea of Henry's opinion on Phil's grave condition by this date: 'I cannot conceive any worse suffering than that which Phil has gone through. It's a great pity that he did not die on the operating table'.

Writing to his father on 24 June 1915, Henry expresses disappointment that his brother Clive is not going to see Phil. Henry apparently had asked Clive to visit Phil as much as possible because he knew 'that my absence would be felt by Phil. Clive and Marjorie seem to have soon forgotten the great kindnesses you and the Mater showed them when their youngsters were so ill'.

Another letter from Henry to his parents a few weeks later sympathises with his parents about the sorrow that would be experiencing: 'Phil's illness has enormously affected the repose in your old age that you had every right to expect'.

However, on 3 September 1915, Henry notes in a letter from his father that Phil's condition had improved markedly. He goes on to say that although rare, it seems that:

> the tumour has spontaneously disappeared or possibly the thorough application of radium by me had a good effect. For some time letters pointed to his being so bad that it seemed useless to write. However I will start to write regularly to him again.

Although by 3 November 1915 on his way to the Western Front in France, Henry wrote:

> Phil must be in a miserable condition and it is a pity that the end cannot come quickly …
>
> …

> As for Phil it is a pity that his sufferings do not end. The sick and wounded in War often suffer a great deal but none in this war suffered as he has.

Sadly, Philip was an invalid for the last two years of his life, dying on 11 August 1916, at forty-one years of age. He was buried in the Balaklava cemetery. It is not known why he was not interred at the Victor Harbor cemetery with other family members. At that time, however, only his grandfather had been buried there, so perhaps his immediate family perhaps saw little reason to do so.

On 2 February 1919, nearly three years after Phil's early death and after leaving British East Africa for good, Victor wrote to his parents from Melbourne. Brother Clive had been killed in South Australia in a dreadful accident, as is explained in Chapter 8. Victor's brotherly love for Phil and also for Clive emerges strongly and poignantly and adds further evidence of the character of these male children of Simpson and Jane's:

> Today is poor old Phil's birthday and I'm afraid that the remembrance must be sad for you, but, after all, he lived a good man's life and it should be some comfort that both he and Clive were men of whom their parents might well be proud. Those of us who remain must try and live up to the traditions you have taught us and, I for one, am proud to be your son and will do all I can to make you proud of me.
>
> Much love to you both from your affectionate son
>
> VM Newland

Sadly little is known about Philip Mesmer Newland, compared with his elder and immediately younger brothers, and he remains something of an unknown quantity. His early life revolved around sport at the highest level, yet there are no details about how he performed as a lawyer. He became the first son of the five to predecease his parents, and his death was cruel and drawn-out. Given what his brothers went on to achieve, it is intriguing to contemplate how his life might have eventuated had he survived for another couple of decades. How might he have contributed to the story of his brothers and the wider family? The answer to this question will never be known.

Given what is known about his early life, it is not unreasonable to assume that he also would have made an impression well beyond the achievements of his first thirty-five years of life. Those of us who have researched his life, including his direct descendants, feel that his shortened life meant the loss of an individual who would likely have amounted to a great deal, bringing honour to both himself and his family, although opinions such as this will forever remain in the realms of speculation.

7

Victor Marra Newland

BORN 18 AUGUST 1876, DIED 12 JANUARY 1953

Of the five sons of Simpson and Jane, Victor is the one whose life stories are the most richly dramatic and awe-inspiring. The family is fortunate to have an extensive record of his achievements, substantially more than those of all of his brothers. This is as much a consequence of his actions as of his thoughts and reflections, which he committed to paper. I have found this something of a surprise. Despite Victor's colourful life, his elder brother Henry is much better known for his remarkable achievements in medicine, as well as for his reputation of being both fearsome and somewhat intimidating, at least to those who knew him more superficially.

In Victor we see a man who seemed to need to prove something and in doing so took on more than most, living his life to the full, including taking many risks in distant lands, participating in wars, pioneering in 'dark' Africa, and all the while displaying courage and persistence, as well as charm and humour. He had a way with women, and with the pen, and was involved in women, shipwrecks, politics and business, and the list goes on.

Victor was christened as Victor Marra, yet his parents referred to him as Marra, as do some of the letters in possession of the family. He understandably did not like this name and avoided its use where possible rather than expunging it altogether out of respect for his parents. Many people, including his brothers, just called him Mick. I will use 'Victor' in this chapter.

Victor was born at Marra station on the Darling River. As with his younger brothers, his early life was one of privilege and comfort, living mostly at Undelcarra and having a decent education, friends and other opportunities reserved largely for the privileged.

As noted earlier, the late Canon Bulbeck wrote a biographical account of Victor's adventures, and in it he referred to Victor's wonderful boyhood horse rides from Undelcarra, in every direction, including the road down to the sea through orchards, market gardens and vineyards. Horsemanship and horse husbandry were expected by his father, who had recognised the importance of decent 'horseflesh'. As with his brothers, Victor took up hunting after he left school. This was to stand him in good stead over subsequent years, where he 'lived and breathed' horses and had to rely on them for survival in conditions many would not be prepared to endure.

Bulbeck refers to two of life's lessons imparted by Victor's parents consistently (possibly too consistently, as can be seen below!) and conscientiously to him and to his brothers: always show consideration for others, but always be strongly independent. These qualities in Simpson and Jane's boys continued to be displayed as they grew from boys to young men, and for those who lived on to older age, becoming men of substance – as their parents had clearly expected – they remained integral to their lives.

Victor's description of himself as a boy, but written by him as an adult, is well worth including in its entirety as it says a lot about what was to come. It is also the first of several letters in which Victor articulates his reflections on humanity and how he might fit, or not:

> I was a rum little beggar as a kid. All fads, sensibilities and imagination. I don't know whether it is safe to generalise from my own case, but even as a child it struck me that parentage meant too much discipline and too little intimacy and confidence. While my material welfare received every care, even to the extent of being pampered, mentally I was in great loneliness. The right and wrong of things was sternly and clearly set out for my instruction. The moral law was laid down, but any enquiry on my part into the mystery of why this was right or that was wrong was dubbed 'naughtiness'. Reason, it seems to me, should be the backbone of discipline and were the children taught the reason for things, boyhood and young manhood would be spared many trials … I developed into a morbid youth – self centred and rebellious. I chafed against well-meant but unexplained bonds and it was only much later that I came to appreciate them. In my early days I wasn't conscious of getting much direction from my Mother, and my Father was almost a stranger to me. I dreaded them both as representing stern authority. I often thought I was disliked … The crown of existence must be a complete love – whether it be for a woman, for one's country, for one's creed or some other worthy pursuit in life. In this search for completeness in love, I early enthroned an ideal of girlhood so sacred as to be practically unapproachable.

According to Bulbeck, Victor once more returned to this theme in his journal many years later, after the Boer War, including also belated credit to his parents:

> This ideal of womanhood, if unattained will turn my aim in life from the pursuit of happiness to that of power. I cannot claim to have lived blamelessly – hot blood will overcome youthful resolution. But, thank God, vice has had no real attraction for me. Damage to my self-respect has always wreaked a punishment beyond the crime ... In my darkest hour my Father retained his faith in me. Once only when I was overwhelmed by failure, did my Mother's wounded pride cry out reproachfully. Both faith and reproach pricked me like a spur and I still do not know which of the two helped me to final success.

That he was prepared to write about the sorts of deep issues he reflected on perhaps explains why Victor chose to take on challenges many would never contemplate, let alone undertake. Exposing himself to the 'slings and arrows of outrageous fortune' and taking risks that few would countenance, he confronted enemy bullets, lions, elephants and African diseases, to name but a few. Surviving all of these things, he lived until he was aged seventy-six, succumbing eventually to the neurological Parkinson's Disease. Given the kinds of activities he'd engaged in during his relatively long life, it is ironic that a neurological condition would end his life rather than a bullet, an elephant or lion, a pestilential disease, drowning or some such violent event. This man willingly chose to experience and live through such events, accompanied along the way by a fair measure of personal faith, about which he had professed self-doubts.

Victor seemed to have been a man of courage, extraordinary luck and good fortune. He also seemed to be a man of humour and remarkable tenderness, given his upbringing and his life experiences. His writings, both in the extensive journal of his early years in Africa and in articles he wrote for newspapers of the day, show what a complex and thoughtful character he really was. Enlisting for the Boer War (without his parents' consent) must have been both rewarding and difficult for him.

However, he seemed to need to prove something to himself as much as to others. He also was keen to gain his parents' approval and love; his letters mention his sadness of not having a sister and what that might have meant for both him and his parents. Someone who is awarded a Military Cross, a Distinguished Conduct Medal and an Order of the British Empire, among other decorations, is not an ordinary sort of person.

Yet something appeared to be missing in Victor's life as a younger man, which may help to explain his commitment to recording his thoughts, as well as his activities. The unsigned account, presumably written by him (it is in very much his style of writing), of the widely known execution of Victor's fellow trooper and friend Harry 'the Breaker' Morant by the British military establishment is documented in its entirety at the end of this chapter. This remarkable piece writing, largely unknown until now, could scarcely fail to move even the most hardened soul. The account provides previously unknown details of this dark application of 'British justice' and, importantly, Victor's assessment of it.

As had his brothers, Victor wanted to be able to prove, to himself, his parents and friends, that he was someone of substance. This desire – almost a need – keeps emerging from his many letters to his parents and his brothers and is further confirmed in his journal and the other records he kept from the time he went to Africa until at least his return to Australia over twenty years later. While in Africa under very trying conditions, Victor retained an extraordinary capacity for optimism, humour, hard work, and a sense of right and honour in his dealings both in war and in peace. He also wanted to demonstrate his 'worthiness', at least to his parents, whom he had struggled to understand as a younger man. He hoped to prove to them and to himself that he was a son of whom they would be proud. In order to achieve this, he deliberately submitted himself to great tests of endurance, courage, financial stress and risk.

Many of these achievements have gone unnoticed until now and it could well be concluded that he is likely to have wanted it that way. Victor did not obviously seek the spotlight; he was a person with a high sense of drive and what might be described as a self-assured and confident attitude. Details about one of his several ventures, Newland, Tarlton & Co (N&T), its genesis as a general agency in 1904 and its eventual success as one of the first 'great white hunter' safari companies, are given later in this chapter. The company still exists under the ownership of Mr Donald Young, a North American originally from Nebraska, who has lived in Kenya for more than thirty years – a worthy testament to Victor over one hundred years later. Five members of the Newland family were fortunate enough to go on safari with Don and his team from Newland, Tarlton & Co. in 2015. This was an emotionally charged and remarkably well-organised experience of a lifetime. As a qualified forensic anthropologist, Don has developed a great interest both in the origins of the company and its South Australian founders. The attention to detail required by him as a forensic anthropologist was also evident in his organisation of our trip, making the several days we had with him most memorable. He and his wonderful team are a modern-day reflection of what it would have been like for those who were able to avail themselves over one hundred years ago of the N&T service. Those of us who had this experience believe that Victor would have been delighted to know, that 111 years after the establishment of the company by him and Leslie Tarlton, some of his descendants took advantage of the current N&T experience in Kenya, an experience that was so much in Victor's blood. It reflected strongly his love for Africa, particularly British East Africa as it was then.

Victor's boyhood life is not documented in the way his early manhood life has been. His two older brothers, Henry and Philip (Phil seems from Victor's letters to have been his favourite), and the two younger brothers, Clive and Ralph, would have participated in typical boys games on the extensive Undelcarra grounds – at that time, about forty acres in the Burnside foothills. Apart from their affluent near neighbours, the Fergusons at Chiverton, other neighbours resided at Urrbrae House, somewhat further away, then owned by the well-known Peter Waite and now by the University of Adelaide and part of the Waite Agricultural Research Institute. Victor was well liked and friendly with many people, especially Effie Ferguson from Chiverton and Lizzie Waite from Urrbrae, both of whom are mentioned in warm terms in his letters. It appears that his interest in girls started reasonably early and, as noted earlier, he laments as a young unmarried man in Africa that he never had a sister. However, he seems to have fantasised about the ideal female as recounted below.

In his journal Victor muses on women and his feelings for them in a passage that gives further insight into this sensitive man, unusual for those late Victorian times:

> So far I feel this record has been lacking in sentiment, and, as a matter of fact, women, except for the merest friendships, until the end of my first stay in Africa, had held no place of consequence in my life. To some this may appear strange, but I attribute this attitude to the fact that as a youngster of ten years I had seen

a little girl who I made up my mind to marry. To her I gave the kind of worship which, I imagine, most children expend on their mothers. I wove fair, even fantastic, dreams around this little damsel until she became such a creature of reverence that I could only approach her with awe.

Once, when we played together by the sea, I knew I might have kissed her, but this strange reverence held me back. I expect she thought I did not care, but it was her fair purity which seemed beyond my touching.

In the years that followed I saw little of her – a glimpse in the street and once I spent an hour at a dance with her, but I was speechless. For a week each Christmas I saw her at the seaside, yet I hardly spoke to her.

When I left for the war she was away. From Africa I occasionally wrote to her and little by little my childhood vow to marry her gathered strength ... There was however another girl correspondent I had gained during the war. She was bright, pretty and witty; her letters were gleams of sunshine during those dark and difficult days. I was looking forward to seeing her also.

On the voyage homeward bound, I flirted with a few passengers and I, who had prided myself on cherishing an ideal of womanhood, found myself getting into a mess.

This however did not change my determination to win my ideal girl. But I found that she did not care and I, ashamed of the love I had made to other women, had no longer the heart to try and attract her. I turned to my other correspondent, for I still felt a warm regard for her charm, her wit and her sympathy. But it was only comradeship that I wanted and she wanted more. I was more than ready to turn my back on Australia and went back to Africa – a wiser man; a common man whose ideals had not stood the strain of worldly realities.

The journal and letters held by Victor's granddaughter Leonie Matheson run from 1899 through to 1925, a period when much was going on in his life. Victor was a regular diarist and prolific letter writer, and it appears from the style and content of his letters that writing was something that he very much enjoyed. Between 1899 and 1905 he wrote an astonishing number of letters to his parents, making me wonder whether he was emulating his father's past letter-writing tendency. Indeed the letter was really the only reasonably reliable form of communication at that time in history and so communication was either by letter or nothing.

As with Simpson's letters, I suspect Victor would be amazed to know that they have become such a source of interest, as well as a means for determining his personality and character. The details given and his choice of language have assisted me to gauge Victor's motivations and to understand how he saw the world around him. As with his older brother Henry, the letters show Victor as a man of bravery, humour, honour and loyalty and also someone with a clear sense of justice and decency. Here was a person who wanted to make his mark, but not in an ostentatious way, but hoping to show his worth as best he could and not at the expense of others.

The letters also indicate that he had a strong streak of humility and filial responsibility and that he was devoted to his parents, particularly to his mother, although not to the exclusion of his father, with whom he had much more business-like relationship. He seemed to long for parental love and approval, emotions which perhaps had not been demonstrated clearly enough by his parents when he was a boy. He occasionally makes mention of these issues in wistful terms. The flow of letters slows down after 1905, when Victor must have been preoccupied with building the Newland, Tarlton & Co business. The letters begin again later, particularly during the latter part of the First World War.

With sixty extremely informative letters, it was hard to resist including all of them, as so many of them are quite absorbing. Indeed, these letters probably deserve publishing in full, although not here, given that this book is about more than purely about Victor.

The first of these letters was written from Urrbrae to Victor's mother on Christmas Day in 1899, when she and Simpson were in England. Only those parts of it that reveal something about him are quoted below. As suggested previously, it is notable that most of the letters in possession of the family are addressed to his mother, with far fewer to his father and brothers. Even though the letter below does not specify that he was spending Christmas Day with the Waites at Urrbrae House, it seems that he was. He was fond of the eldest of Peter Waite's daughters, Lizzie, who is mentioned briefly in some of his letters:

> Urbrrae
> 25/12/99
> My Dearest Mother.
>
> Christmas Day with heat and dust, but a nice cool house and kind friends. You will be surprised to learn that before you get this I will be en route for England via the Cape – in other words I am coming home to see you after putting in a few months fighting the Boers. I am feeling an awful brute for the trouble I am going to cause you, but you must be brave and not think that anything is going to happen to me, for after all I am young and strong, the chances of bullets are small and the hard life will make a man of me. I am sure next time you see me I will be not be pale faced and soft, but brown and fit for anything ... Try not to look at the dark side of things – think of the chances I am getting, and how fit and

strong the experience will make me – I know I am not treating you fairly, flying off without your consent, but when you left, I had never dreamed of what was before me. I am in for it now, however, and but for the thought of your sorrow, would be glad. I will try to fight like a true soldier and as a son of so good a mother should do: I am sober and steady and will always try to be a credit to you who have done so much for me. Dearest love to you all and – 'au revoir'.

Your affec son

VM Newland

His sense of optimism, perhaps even naivety, about the opportunities the war will give him and the need to prove himself are clearly apparent.

Victor Marra Newland as mounted trooper in 1899.
[Photo courtesy Leonie Matheson]

Although he did not seek the permission of his parents before leaving for South Africa, he clearly wanted to show himself as worthy of his famous father and his heritage. The following postscript from his second letter, dated 21 January 1900, to his mother presents him as seeking filial approval: 'Please give my love to the dear old Pater and ask him not to worry about me: I will try to do my duty over there and show myself a son worthy of him'.

Victor's next very informative letter is from the ship on which he sailed from Australia for Africa and in part describes what he experienced and what he thought of his departure:

> SS Surrey
> 29/1/00
> My dearest Mother
>
> Here we now are fairly out at sea in the Bight with our vessel putting her nose into the waves in good style. This is no passenger boat and our decks are not like P&O's. Both for [sic] and aft along the bulwarks are horse stalls each just giving room for a horse to stand, but of course without a chance of lying down. There are three tiers of stalls, the lowest down on the bilge, always close and hot and in parts pitch dark. During yesterday and last night I spent 8 hours down there – nearly everyone who went down was sick but I escaped. It is well worth while to put in a spell in such a place for the pleasure one gains from a whiff of fresh air on getting up to deck … You will see from the papers what a magnificent enthusiasm the people of Adelaide showed as we paraded through the streets prior to our departure: it was something to be remembered to the end of a man's life … dozens of girls along the line held up their faces to be kissed, but the restiveness of my horse would not permit of such luxuries: it was

dreadfully sad at times of course, but taken all together I have never seen anything so inspiring.

All the way down to Pt Adelaide it was just the same. One unknown damsel rushed out and presented me with a silver sword brooch as a keepsake. Lizzie Waite has proved a perfect Briton to me. I can't imagine a better friend; she presented me with an awfully nice silver pencil before we started …

The photograph in Leonie Matheson's possession (Victor's paternal granddaughter) highlights the imposing figure that Victor in a mounted trooper's uniform and on his horse must have presented. This, combined with his apparently energetic, even swashbuckling, personality indicates that, as with his elder brother Phil, who was the closest to him in age, he was not short of charm. The people of Adelaide are fortunate to have a remarkably fine statue of a trooper on horseback – the Boer War memorial – outside the main gates of Government House. The uniform Victor wears in his photograph is strikingly similar to that on the memorial, but Victor was lucky enough to survive the conflict.

A letter is to his father two weeks later is relatively matter-of-fact and includes a comment about inter-colonial rivalry:

SS 'Surrey'
17/2/00
My dear Father,

Here we are now within measurable distance of the Cape … I certainly never thought 3 months ago that I was ever going to do such hard work as I have done on board this boat, but all the same I have got dreadfully fat and feel grand. I soon got sick of sleeping on the troop deck – I now always sling my hammock in the open air and enjoy fresh air and good sleep ... We had a grand tug of war between the different Colonies last week – of course SA won but our team had to work all right. We had some spar-boxing as well. I have beaten two men and am in the final, to be decided shortly ... We have frequent concerts on board, and there is great rivalry between the Colonies as to which shall give the best. We lead easily ... Most of us Adelaide chaps have put on weight on board but the life does not seem to suit the bushmen with us. I hope both you and Mother are enjoying the cool climate and are well. I wonder how Clive and Hal are getting on. My word, home letters will be appreciated. Love to all;

From your affec son

VM Newland

The reality of war and the dreadful conditions increasingly confronting the Australian troopers are apparent in the letter to Philip reproduced in the previous chapter. Once again, the spirit of optimism and Victor's cheerful acceptance of circumstances come through, no matter how bad.

In a letter to his mother he writes in a most offhand way about his swim in the Orange River, which led to his award of the Distinguished Conduct Medal (DCM):

In Train for Bloemfontein
29/3/1900
My dearest Mother,

We returned yesterday from a 250 mile ride to Prieska and back and now on our way to join Lord Roberts' forces at Bloemfontein from which place we are to try and make our way to Pretoria. Our Prieska ride was very rough, but we Australians beat the Britishers and got first into the town – I would not have missed

> the last 10 miles headlong going for anything. The Boers fled before across the Orange River taking the punt across with them. Two of us volunteered to swim across and bring her back – the current was awfully strong and I went down once and thought it was all up – I am glad I went though, it was a great experience …

A day later a letter to his father was much more prosaic. Victor fails to mention in this letter that his dangerous and almost fatal swim across the Orange River was the key reason for his being awarded the Distinguished Conduct Medal; his humility appears to be on display. His natural optimism, possibly lack of experience, is apparent: he mentions the war finishing soon, while history shows that it dragged on for another two years. The letter gives a clear hint about what a future in Africa might bring for him

The topic of money, to enable him to establish some future business venture is mentioned, and, from what can be gathered from later letters, Simpson appeared quite prepared to help. However, despite the offer of financial help, it seems that Victor wanted to make his own way in a country that he thought would provide many opportunities after the war had finished. Perhaps somewhat prematurely, he was also keen to have his father's opinion of those potential opportunities:

> Norval's Pont
>
> 1/4/1900
>
> My dear Father,
>
> The Boers having blown up the bridge over the Orange River we have been blocked here for two days – tomorrow we cross by pontoon and make our way by short stages to Bloemfontein. Now that the War is so nearly at an end, I think I ought to let you know what my plans are. Since arriving in this country, I have seen clearly that storekeeping is and will be a most paying game for

the next few years. I will get my discharge at Capetown and take out a storekeeper's license at once – Leo Henderson coming in with me. I don't intend to stick at one place, but to shift with the population. Once started and with a little capital much money can be made in other directions. Henderson is a brewer and we might do something in that way – many Boer farms will be confiscated and offered by auction (men who know the land say its value will increase threefold under British management) – lastly there are hundreds of goldfields which Kruger has suppressed and from these alone we ought to do well in the way of stores. I have said what I intend doing, but of course much depends on what you say. I will have about 175 pounds cash here at Seawright & Co., Capetown, by the time the war is over – I can of course make a start on that, but, if you care to risk the money, I reckon with 500 pounds, I could do really well. Profits at present are tremendous and though I like my present life, I can't help wishing that I had come storekeeping not soldiering.

Your affec son

VM Newland

The next excerpt is from a letter to brother Philip and clearly indicates that Victor wanted to ensure he had his parents' approval for his departure for Africa to fight in the Boer War, despite not waiting for their consent. His concern accords with his attitude toward his parents and his desire to be a good son and one they could be proud of. He shares this feeling with his favourite brother and then, a day later, more formally with his father, where the tone of his letter is very much one of wanting to be a son worthy of such a father, but also someone who is prepared to volunteer for risky deeds that others quite reasonably might not want to take on:

Bloemfontein
11/4/1900
My dear Phil,

Arrived here yesterday, were humbugged about a lot and at last got into camp and got our letters. No one who has not been thro' the mill can realise what it means to get letters after one has had none for 3 weeks. The Mater and Pater write as if they were quite proud of my coming – thank goodness for of it [*sic*] – I was awfully afraid they might be offended.

Bloemfontein
12/4/1900
My dear Father

Your kind letters make me feel more than I have ever felt what good parents I have for a while cut myself off from. I am glad you think I have acted rightly and you may be sure I will try to be worthy of my Father. Our fighting work is yet to come – so far we have only endured the hardships of our flying march to Prieska – one of the swiftest of the company, and the discomforts incidental to ordinary marching. I fully realise the dangers before me and have every intention of adopting the cautious tactics in vogue here – viz. be flat and use all cover but I feel certain that if volunteers are wanted for dangerous work, you would expect me to step out. We Australians are wonderfully lucky and I have not the slightest fear of getting hurt. Your remarks re. money are very kind indeed – probably 25 pounds will see me thro' the campaign – little luxuries such as bread, butter and jam are very dear. Bread 1 shilling a loaf, jam 2 shillings a tin and so on. I have already said that much money will be made here after the War – I am simply longing to get back to friends and home – out here one is cut off from all that makes the joy of life, but Mammon must be

satisfied – with your permission I will make a start here and then do a flying trip home.
Love from yr affec son
VM Newland'

The extraordinary flow of letters to his parents and brothers all highlight Victor's capacity to accept whatever might lie before him, no matter how unpleasant and dangerous the circumstances. The contrast between his comfortable life at Undelcarra and the risks out in the South African veldt under enemy fire could scarcely be greater. Yet he sees benefit in experiencing tough conditions and developing self-reliance, characteristics he believes will make him a man, as well as impress his parents, thus being worthy of his family heritage, as he saw it. Writing about the war to *The Register* newspaper was apparently something he took on as well:

Bloemfontein
12/4/1900
My dearest Mother,

You can have no idea how – ever since leaving Adelaide I have looked forward to receiving letters from you both and hearing what you think of my going soldiering. The night before last we rode into this place and got our mails before turning in – I am awfully delighted to hear that you both think I have done right – don't be too anxious – I am fit and well and after all the danger from bullets is very slight. You are right in saying that I have realised how many comforts I have left behind – if ever I want to call up an ideal of happiness I think of dear old Undelcarra, parents, brothers, cosy meals with good tea, jam and cream, kind friends and everything to make life enjoyable. I turn to the contrast here, hard work, poor tucker and often little of it, bare ground to sleep on and blankets frequently wet and wonder what there is to attract in such life – yet I do like it with its varying experiences and great possibilities … last night we had a tremendous thunderstorm one of the loudest I have ever heard – we were lying out in the rain all night without shelter and with blankets soon soaked through – you can imagine what a comfort both sweater and night cap were – my legs were the only part of me to get wet and despite the rain I was only kept awake for a few minutes in all. I put on a pair of the socks this morning – they are great … I received 22 letters and about the same number of papers as my share of the mail – so you will see I am well supplied with news – Lizzie Waite and little Effie Ferguson turned out bricks and wrote several long letters – I had one from 'The Register' expressing great satisfaction with my first letter to them and hoping to get many more … a cake would go grandly – we never see such a thing here.

Stamps on envelope are valuable – Clive would like them – tell him to write.

Victor's capacity and acceptance to take in his stride whatever is served up to him is certainly evident in the next letter, although perhaps some of it might have been bravado to impress his father; yet, given what Simpson endured at Marra and other places in the bush, this seems less likely. Victor seems to want to show that he can cope with whatever he has to confront with humour and a sense almost of fatalism:

Bloemfontein
14/4/00
My dear Father,

I am writing in a little humpy made of Henderson's and my horse blankets – ever since my last letter we have had awfully wet weather and consequently discomfort. Overnight 65 of us were out on outlying picket on kopjes round here. We slept amongst some low bushes and though my blankets and overcoat got simply drenched I slept like a top until my turn of duty came, only waking up once or twice when the thunder and lightning were worse than usual. I do nothing but laugh at the misadventures of some of the other chaps – really the game is not half bad if one can joke over it ... It is marvellous how well we have all kept considering our hardships and bad food: often lately I have made my meals of bread and fat, sometimes fried. Yesterday I bought a 1lb tin of jam for 2 shillings and was mighty glad to get it: a pound of biscuits costs me the same price, so that money goes a very little way here. I am getting 10 pounds up from the Cape as I am 'broken' ... Our horses now get a chance to lie down or move about in camp: they are tied head to head about a yard apart – the poor brutes look miserable and are losing condition. There is none of the glitter and glory of war about what we have done so far – it is simply a case of enduring the life to make a man hard and self reliant. Already I feel older with a broader view of things that when I lived in Adelaide. Goodness knows! I will be glad enough to get back to home and happiness, but such a life as this cannot but do good to a fellow rapidly becoming narrow minded in little Adelaide – I feel indeed now that life is opening and hard work it is. It is sad to feel that our old home is getting so broken up – please God, it will not be very many months before I get a chance to do a flying trip to Australia ... Hope both you and the Mater are having a good time – it must be nice to have old Hal with you sometimes.

Love to all, from your affec son

VM Newland

The news of the likely sale of Undelcarra, as mentioned in the letter following, appears to come as more of a blow to Victor than the war situation, of which he is part. Clearly his boyhood home meant a lot to him. He also has some amusing remarks from afar about his brothers and their female companions; the latter he may well be missing himself. However, it seems very likely that he was charmingly sharing experiences by correspondence with various Adelaide female friends, although there is no clear evidence of this in any of the family records:

> Karree's Kloof
> 1/5/1900
> My dearest Mother and Father,
>
> I have this morning returned from 2 days picket on Loyal Kopje – the key of our position here – from which place I got the most magnificent panoramic view of a battle it is possible to conceive ... Our little picket on the kopje were successful in running off with 2000 pounds worth of beef and mutton from right under the Boers' eyes. You can imagine my delight this morning in getting my letters and parcel – by Jove! that cake tasted good after not having had anything of the sort for so long. The other things are just what a fellow wants and now I feel that I will be able to get on grandly in the hard marches and work before us. I am awfully sorry that the Pater seems to think of selling Undelcarra. To get back to Adelaide without the dear old home to go to would be dreadful ... would it not be better to let rather than sell – for goodness sake, don't do the latter. Ralph has written me a most amusing letter – if ever a chap is happy he is – with his horseriding, many friends and Hazel – he has asked me for a battlefield curio for her, certainly they are easily enough

got. It is only 3 days since I last wrote, but tomorrow we go into action and in view of that I think it is as well to give all the news I can now. By the by Phil is not attached to Jo, it is to Miss Bessie, who unluckily for him, does not reciprocate. It is this I think that makes Phil a bit down – it is very silly of him to be so despondent. We have been feeding well the last day or two and it is a good preparation for the work ahead. Our fellows yesterday won the admiration of the British officers – they fought like bricks and in the retreat were as cool as possible – one of them, Balfour-Ogilvy got off his horse under fire to give a dismounted comrade a spell and Billy Gosse rode in under a hot fire to dress the wounds of the fallen. I will try and send you some African bulbs soon – they are very beautiful. I have written this letter basking naked in the sun after a good swim – I feel fit and grand and am confident of getting through well. Don't be anxious on the score of healthy, I'll be all right. The greatest luxury you could send me would be a box of sweets which are unobtainable here – they may not reach me, but done up in a soldered tin box there would be a fair chance – good bye my dear parents, all love and best wishes for good health and happiness to you. Don't sell the old place and don't worry about Phil – he is all right only a bit fidgety.

Yours affec

VM Newland

The next letter describes well how he and his fellow troopers coped with real action under fire and also how the results of war affected Boer women caught up in such dreadful circumstances. This theme of concern for those who might be regarded by some as part of 'the enemy' appears again later:

Kronstadt
13/5/00

My dearest Mother and Father,

Here we are safely arrived at the temporary capital of the Free State, our entrance being made without resistance at the end. Since last writing, I have been in four engagements and now know what it is to hear the bullets whiz around me and the shells scream and burst. The first fight I got into was the worst, though the bad only lasted a few minutes – it was during our attack on Brandtfort. A party of us were in a creek taking refuge from the shells when some Boers began firing on us from a farm looking down on the run of the creek – with the banks on either hand to guide them they made good practice and by Jove we had narrow shaves – the horse next to me was shot and bullets came all around – four of us lay down on the bank and replied, silencing their fire for a while, but they soon began again and we had to get (sic). As we mounted I dropped my rifle and had to get off to pick it up. I don't pretend to be brave, and frankly confess that the beastly shells made me think of home and wonder if I should be hit, but to see the other fellows clear made me laugh like anything – one chap got his reins caught in his horse's legs and looked the picture of horror when he had to dismount and free them: another could not mount a restive horse – two or three others pulled up to help him and I stopped for a minute – he had lost his presence of mind and was saying 'It's no use – I can't get up – I'll have to stop' – in piteous tones. By Jove! The sergeant major did round on him and fairly frightened him on to the moke. Farther on, fellows were riding all out, as if in a race and in front of one, over one, behind one, the bullets fell harmlessly. The fray went on from midday to dark and as you have of course heard, we rolled the Boers back. The next three days were but a repetition of the first except that we got into very little rifle fire, the artillery doing practically everything. In the last fight we had I went to sleep lying on my face behind an anthill with two of our pompoms 50 yards away firing over my head and the enemy's shell replying. We had a good deal of rifle fire at us that day also and I was awakened by hearing the bullets ping close at hand. We were acting as escort to two pompoms and had to lie in the grass from 1 to 6 – with 3.30 and 4 am reveilles we nearly all slept … It is heart rending at times to see the Boer women in their homes eyes full of tears and a break in their voice as we speak to them – thank goodness our fellows are comparatively gentle and I have seen them give rough brutes fits at times. I have just had a great swim in the river here and could not feel better – you can imagine that without blankets, and bitterly cold nights, our sleep on the march here has not been all bliss

Love to you both from both Charlie and self, and wishing the Mater a very happy birthday.

I remain your affec son
VM Newland

The harsh impacts of war on Boer families is further described by Victor in the next letter, five days later, and displays his admiration for their coping in such difficult circumstances, combined with feelings of sympathy for them. Victor faithfully records an incident involving a young Boer girl with 'flashing eyes'. This event appeared to have a strong impact on him, notwithstanding what he has suffered himself. For anyone, particularly a young Africaner girl, standing her ground and saying what she said under the circumstances of that time represented a courageous act. The letter also reveals sympathy and some of Victor's feelings of guilt:

Kronstadt
18/5/00
My dearest Mother and Father,

We yesterday returned from a 3 day's disarming patrol round the farms of the neighbourhood. It has been very good fun, though it is on such missions that one catches a glimpse of the great sadness of war, where homes (had to adjourn here, being sent out on mounted picket for the night) – to continue – are burnt down for concealment of arms – where deepest black tells of father or brothers slain, or sullen reserve, of his absence at the front. One listens with pity the tales of utter ruin – no flour, no milk – Arms? Oh certainly not! We walk in and pull things about a bit and find a Mauser and many rounds of ammunition. That is the worst of it – one can never believe what he hears, but still I sometimes feel awfully mean when I am stealing my dinner from a poultry yard and hear the plaintive cry 'I am only a poor woman – O please leave me my fowls!' Still we must live and in such a great army as this, we would fare badly if we depended on our rations and you will no doubt understand that a tender duck or chicken, to say nothing of fresh eggs, butter and milk, are great temptations. At one house the mother and elder daughters were mutely passive, but the youngest girl faced the troop of us pluckily with flashing eyes – 'you English take all from us', she said 'our fathers, our flour, our fowls – and now you are taking our country'. We of course told her that the war would soon be over and they would be better off than ever. 'I hope so, I hope so', she said, but was evidently very doubtful …

In a letter of 28 May 1900 Victor is still displaying his optimism and endurance, despite the risky circumstances in which he finds himself. Also interesting in the letter is the description of some of the day-to-day activities of the life of a soldier – including details of the food he was cooking and eating. Also evident is his understated humour, particularly his accounts of a couple of a near-misses in incidents involving horses

28/5/00
Georgetown (10 miles past Johannesburg)
My dearest Father and Mother,

A week yesterday we left Kronstadt – it has been a week of hard work, long hours and hardship, through which, however, I have come out in grand health … we are often in action, but the foe always flee before we get at them and except for a passing shell or a chance bullet we meet with no danger … An hour we lie half asleep in grass up to our horses' shoulders and then as nightfall comes we are told to get back to camp – a nice game with holes everywhere and rough drifts to cross. We move on in the darkness and get over about half the distance by the help of much spurring – then comes the order just as we have crossed a nasty drift – 'return to another camp on the wing you are returning from' – we curse and go back. By nine o'clock after much muddling and fussing we are in camp – we kill a few sheep – give our mounts 4 lbs of mealies and have our tea of fried meat and Johnny cakes prepared by my self – then I decide to celebrate our entry into the Transvaal by making a cake – the ingredients – flour, condensed milk, sugar, baking powder, suet and raisins. I bake it or rather fry it in fat – most successful and greatly appreciated next day. I turn in at 1230 and have hardly gone to sleep when the Captain nudges me 'Get up, it is 2 o'clock and we are off at 4'. What a shock! Had never dreamt we would move before 6. Cold, frosty morning – waterbags hard – ground white and crackling under the horses' hoofs as we move. Then comes another wearying day – horses dead tired … This brings me up to date and to this town, where I am one of a guard of four on a hotel looted alike by Boer and British. I am in comfort unknown for months, last night sleeping on a spring mattress with Charlie Butler and having an old Hindoo to clean up the rooms and make tea or cook anything for us. Breakfast and dinner have been perfect meals at a Mrs Kelly's boarding house – clean linen and cutlery and beautiful food – porridge, stew, eggs, new bread, butter and jam for breakfast and soup, steak and kidney pie, rice pudding and fruit, new milk, tea and hot bread for dinner. Mrs Kelly, an elderly woman who must have been very beautiful when younger, who will not take a penny in payment – awfully good of her, wasn't it with provisions as dear as they are here. You will see that I am not living badly – in fact, I weigh well over 12 stone – tomorrow we move on to Pretoria and by the end of the week I hope to be able to cable you from there that I am safe and well. My luck has certainly been in so far, as my horse turned a somersault with me the other day and fairly flattened me out without injury, though everyone thought I was killed. Again, the other day I slung my rifle across my back – a thing I rarely do – and I'm bothered if Charlie Butler's horse did not choose the occasion to kick at me, only the rifle saving me from a tremendous blow on the back. At this game one meets many fine fellows – men with titles roughing it with the rest of us and turning out good men …

Love to you both and all good wishes

From your affect son

VM Newland

The dangers for mounted troopers are reiterated in the letter below, but this letter also contains reflections of a more personal nature: he reminisces fondly about Undelcarra and his life there, and comments on the charming letters he has received from his retinue of female correspondents:

> Esterfaken
> 14 miles E Pretoria
> 13/7/1900
> My dearest Mother and Father,
>
> I had my horse wounded in the leg on patrol a few days ago – we got it very hot from 3 sides at once at short range, but escaped without injury. You will see there is little need for anxiety as regards bullets, seeing that we were without cover and were in a clump firing with our arms through our bridle reins. Our Australian luck is wonderful … Effie Ferguson – who writes me the sweetest and kindest of letters – seems usually to be able to tell which are mine … I am glad to think that out here I am pretty sure to be able to battle along for myself with a fair chance of doing really well. I do not intend to ask for any home help if I can help it – as it seems to me that nothing can be better for a young fellow than to have to trust entirely to his own wits. Certainly as soon as I can afford it I will revisit dear old Undelcarra – I appreciate now in a way I never did before my parents and home. I have also found out my best friends – Lizzie Waite and Effie have written me every mail and I am writing this with a cartridge pencil sent me by the former. Marion Ayers, Katie Lingley (now Moore) the other Chiverton folk and Mr Cooper have also sent me the nicest of letters … What a jolly good thing it is Ralph becoming such an enthusiastic horseman – what can't a girl do? I confess there are often times when I feel I would like to be back with you all – to hear a bit of Chiverton music, ride a bicycle and try to punch out a rail or so after the hounds – yet after all this

is the best game a fellow can play and the 'afterwards' will more than make up for any dangers and hardship.
Love to you all from your affec son
VM Newland

This next excerpt continues in a similar and entertaining vein and, as with most of his letters, is full of interesting information about his activities. Noticeably, among his quite varied activities, he enjoys cooking:

29/6/00
Botha's Farm 22 miles beyond Pretoria
My dearest Mother,

We were all highly delighted a couple of days ago at the arrival of a mail – two having been burnt – the third having escaped. The flannel shirt also arrived, but the socks, I am afraid, decorate the feet of some Boer. I hope you did not curtail your English visit on my account. I had looked forward to seeing you in London, as it appears we are likely to go there when the war is over. It is my intention to look round this country before returning to live in Australia, but if I get a government billet I shall apply for 3 months leave almost at once to take a trip and see you all again. I shall really have to fast or do something to get my fat off – I am getting enormous everyone says – certainly I could not feel better. Both myself and horse being fit, I get in for nearly all patrols – you would be surprised how quickly we can turn out when the Boers are sighted and volunteers wanted to go at them – in 4 minutes we are in the saddle and away. Yesterday when on patrol I commandeered a fine fat duck and, today being off duty by way of a change, I decided to celebrate the occasion by roasting it – accordingly we dined off roast duck with bread, onion and chilli seasoning, followed by mealie bread and dripping with cheese and tea. Dinner over I made a roley poley pudding, now boiling, completing the operation by licking the jam tin clean and when I have written this letter, I am going to make oyster patties for tea, using a tin of oysters we have carried since Bloemfontein.

In the next two excerpts we see Victor reflecting on what he hopes to do when he no longer is soldiering. As we saw earlier, he envisages many opportunities and feels confident about his capacity to make something of his life as a civilian, but little does he know how hard it will be. Once again, we see that an offer of financial assistance has been made by his father:

Doorn Kop
9/8/00

My dear Father,

Many thanks for your two letters received last mail and for your offers of financial assistance, should I require it. In a life like this there is so much uncertainty and every day brings so many apparent opportunities before a fellow that he never knows what he really intends to do at any future date. My present intention is to go to England with the troops – spend as much time as I can spare with merchant houses, so as to get known and then return here – to Johannesburg or thereabouts and chance my luck as business openings occur … Certainly there will be splendid chances soon for the fellow with the skill to seize them.

Wunderfontein
22/8/00

My dear Father and Mother,

… By the by am going to write Mr Reynell on the subject of trade with Australia in wine and sheep – no doubt, he will kindly help me in the matter – I may ask for the agency of the Adelaide Wine Co, but it will be time enough to write you fully when safely out of this ...

The next letter from Victor, written over four days, gives a great deal of information about the Boer War and the fighting conditions, which makes its inclusion in its entirety relevant. It is also notable for its writing style, particularly the last part, where he dramatically describes the 'wolf gnawing within'. The conditions the men faced may go some way to explaining why Victor eventually ended up with health and nerves problems, probably what is now known as Post-Traumatic Stress Disorder (PTST), which led to his enforced return to Australia in 1922:

Belfast

28/8/00

My dear Father and Mother,

I am writing this in a silver wattle plantation where I have been sitting alongside my horse, half sleeping for nearly four hours, before that lying flat on the veldt under a burning sun waiting for a small party of Boers that fired a few shots and ran. The pompom some our fellows were escorting fired between 300 and 500 shots yesterday afternoon and has been going strong all day – of course this will have drawn much fire on them and I am wondering if all are safe – report says not. I'm beginning to feel a great craving for meat, having had none since yesterday morning – it is now 5 o'clock. Yesterday was one of the most awful we have had – a cutting wind, sweeping dirt along with it until we all looked like sweeps and were chilled to the very bone – it was after dark when we got into camp and after eating some biscuit porridge, turned in – water froze one and a half inches thick in the night, but, thank goodness, I slept warm – no rheumatism. It is simply grand the Boers making a stand – we should soon finish them off now. (Will continue this when I get time).

29/8/00

This is the fourth day since I made a halt in my letter, days full of excitement such as the rest of the campaign has not afforded. The first was merely picket work with an accompaniment of sniping, we continuing to protect the left flank. We remained on the veldt all night and a little party of us rode into camp for fodder, blankets and food, for we had none. It was pitchy black and we had to pass through much bog – on the way back my horse got caught in barbed wire, threw me and nearly rolled over me – fox holes were plentiful and twice I came a purler in these, always unhurt however. Next morning the marshy country was a wonderful picture of icicles, but we had little leisure for admiration of these starting with the light on a patrol —- With a rattle and rush we took J battery out from cover into a perfect hail of bullets – three times she tried to get into position in vain – no man could face the fire, and then we got her into action at 400 yards from the enemy – it was grand to ride as we rode laughing at death – a chap wanted to cheer and tell the beggars to come on – so much will a galloping horse and rattling accoutrements do. The Guards came behind us on foot nothing like the mark we were, yet in a few minutes, 27 of them went down and we were scathless. I was in charge of an escort to one of the pompoms – we were only three all told – so hot was the fire that we were outnumbered(?) under cover and ran the gun into position by hand – talk about done – I was dead to the world, but we soon got into action and between five o'clock and dark poured in about 200 shells. A chap had but to kneel up and a hail of bullets came at him. Our colonel sent for reinforcements but there were none, and so we fought on. Until after dark we stayed there then withdrew to camp, the Boers firing the grass behind us to harass our movements and a glorious night it was – practically no tucker, a few hours' sleep, and again we were in the saddle and under fire – not rifles this time, but shrapnel that followed us as we went again and again bursting overhead just missing us – two unlucky Warwicks got what was meant for us – mortal wounds. Then all day long we lay on a stony ridge half sleeping or watching French's cavalry charge a kopje on our left where they drove in the Boer flank. All day shell thundered and burst but we were unmolested, whilst Buller on our right – ran his guns up within 1000 yards of the foe and drove them from their trenches. At night we bivouacked on the ground we had won – had a frugal tea and turned in, whilst the clouds specked rain and threatened us with further discomfort. Now we are halted at the base of a rocky ridge waiting to finish the fray, for the Boers are retreating northward to Lydenburg and must engage us soon – we have got them all right but the fight will be hard – hope to goodness our Australian luck continues. My hands are black with the filth of three days – my eyes seem half clogged and the wolf is gnawing within me, but we are all in good heart and looking forward to what the day will bring forth.

Love to you all from your very dirty and unshaven, but affectionate son,
VM Newland
The whistle has just sounded we move and the fun begins.

The end of Victor's service in the Boer War was a time of further tribulation for him, with what is described by him and recorded in Bulbeck's biographical account, as 'standing camps, endless friction with authority, reviews and complimentary addresses from homebound Generals'. Interestingly, he is more fulsome in his journal, probably written retrospectively, in his middle age. The section about women is particularly revealing, principally about Victor himself:

> Looking back now, that year of war service seems the happiest time of my life. It had brought me into close communication with my parents; it had given me an experience of men such as I could never have gained in days of peace. I know the knowledge gained was primitive, but nevertheless it was fundamental to the understanding of fellowship … Living daily with the roughest and toughest of men I learnt that danger and hardship do much to bring out unselfishness. You find, as a matter of course, the bold man taking the place of danger from the timid; the strong man relieving the weak; hungry men sharing their meagre rations with their mates. I have even seen panic-stricken man wait under fire for his laggard pal to catch up. I have known cases of fear and failure, but when the greed for gold is absent, I have found that the good always seems to outweigh the evil …
>
> Women? Can women ever realise how much it means to men to feel their influence? Keep in touch with your menfolk whether present or absent – it will pay you rich dividends soon or late. I know what the friendship of good women has meant to me. If I have failed to live up to my ideals, their friendship has helped me struggle back, and to seek the best again. I have also seen what the absence of a woman's influence has meant to many luckless devils.

The following excerpt yet again challenges the claim that Victor's father Simpson was endlessly 'penny-pinching'. There is little doubt that Simpson used his money wisely and he certainly had no intention of squandering it unnecessarily on his children; Simpson expected them to make their own way in life. That does not mean that he was ungenerous where he thought it appropriate. The letter below indicates that generosity and certainly Victor was not going to take advantage of his father's generosity if he felt he did not need to:

> Botha's Farm
> 29/6/00
> My dear Father,
>
> I was awfully delighted to receive the day before yesterday your kind letter written just before your departure from England. It is very good of you to allow me to draw up to 500 pounds, if I require it for business purposes – should I ask you for the money I will do my very best to use it well and profitably ...

Dated 20 April 1901, one of the many letters Simpson wrote to Henry includes in part clear recognition of Victor's drive to achieve and succeed:

> Marra writes he is staying on in Africa & I commend his pluck & endurance & seriously hope he will meet with the reward he merits. Most of his Corps, the second contingent, are on the way back & it must have been a hard tug for him to allow them to return without him ...

The life Victor decided to attempt for himself by remaining in Africa after his war service was not easy. By the end of the Boer War, in 1902, he was twenty-five years old and his letters show that he had endured the hardships probably better than most, even though he was to pay the price later. It could be that his decision to stay was a consequence of the expectations of his parents and his need to prove that he was indeed a 'real' man in his father's eyes. Whatever the reasons, I believe it was likely that both the Boer War and his later experiences during the First World War exacted a higher toll from Victor than he and others, such as his parents, realised. He may well have suffered from a degree of 'shell shock', or PTST, at the time not fully recognised for what it was, as subsequent events, recounted below, indicate. Over the next several years, he embarked on various ventures from shopkeeping to agency work, to trading in wine and sheep, all the while being occasionally tempted by government jobs. He saw the gold-mining industry and the need for stores and equipment as an opportunity, noting that his youngest brother Ralph had come to South Africa in 1904 as a mining engineer. It is understood that Ralph stayed in South Africa for at least a couple of years from that date.

Victor made a trip of several weeks back to Adelaide at the end of 1901. As his journal recounts:

> I spent five hectic weeks among relatives and friends, and then I was at sea again, bound for Africa on the SS *Warrigal.* I had dreams of fortune in my mind, for my sentimental journey was over, but bitter disillusionment awaited me. For the first five months after my return in 1902, I remained in government service, but whilst in Australia I had determined to leave it and had arranged for my appointment as Commissioner of Trade and Affidavits by the South Australian Government. The promises made to me by the heads of my department were broken and I put in my resignation, expressing the hope when doing so, that they would soon find government service as irksome as I did.

Victor's attempts at commercial and general brokering were only partially successful. He worked hard for little reward and found the interactions with so-called partners quite disillusioning. From reading his account, it seems he expected honesty from his colleagues and for commitments to be maintained. This was his modus operandi, which, he discovered, was not regularly reciprocated. By way of example, he lent what little money he had to people purportedly in need and, as he said, his faith in human nature was badly shaken when the debt was 'dishonoured'.

In 1904, during this low point in his life, he met Leslie Tarlton, who also came from South Australia, and his family, who as a whole, showed him much kindness, partly restoring his faith in human nature. His journal gives a wonderful, albeit somewhat less than complimentary, description of someone with whom he was destined to spend so much time over the next several years:

> It was just when things were at their worst that Leslie Tarlton came into my life. The truest of friends and yet one of the most unprepossessing men I hever known. This queer figure of a little man, knock-kneed, hollow-chested, huge head crowned with red hair, eyes white-lashed, upper lip completely hidden by a heavy red moustache – of such a mould was Leslie J. Tarlton, once of South Australia, a trooper in the war, secretary of companies, a man with a big spirit in a little body – the ugliest, pluckiest and truest man it has ever been my good fortune to meet. His ungainly, awkward manner and large head on an ill-formed body; his white eyelashes and flaming hair for a time repelled me – I felt far more dislike than friendship. But even that ugly husk could not conceal for ever his great and magnanimous nature. It is true that over the years there were times when we fought and mistrusted each other, but we learnt thoroughly each other's virtues and

failings and long before the end of our association I knew him for the most loyal, true-hearted friend I was ever to possess.

The name Tarlton appears in South Australia's history in the latter part of the nineteenth century. The Hon. R.A. Tarlton was a member of the Legislative Council for about eighteen years and a contemporary of Victor's father Simpson. It is highly likely that Leslie Tarlton was a relative of R.A. Tarlton, probably a son, although that connection has not been clearly established. Historical records show that an R.A. Tarlton had strong views about England's very definite role in subjugating the Boers in the Boer War. He was residing in South Africa in 1904 when Victor and Leslie Tarlton developed their business partnership.

R.J. Cunninghame, Victor Newland, Leslie Tarlton and Alan Black in 1909.
[Photo courtesy Donald Young of Nairobi,
current owner of Newland, Tarlton Co. (N&T)]

Leslie Tarlton offered advice to Victor on his current business arrangements, which had left Victor broken in both pocket and spirit, and assisted him to extricate himself. Victor's journal indicates that at this time, astonishingly and notwithstanding his optimistic personality, he contemplated suicide as the most honourable action. Only reproachful letters from his mother, and another, warm with sympathy from the girl of his dreams, seemed to pull him back from the brink.

Victor and Tarlton decided to try their fortunes in Uganda, as the country around Lake Victoria, according to Victor, was 'vaguely' called; in actual fact it was the Uganda Protectorate or part of British East Africa. This was the start, in 1904, of the Newland, Tarlton & Co. venture, which was to occupy both men until after the start of the First World War; they were largely working from the fledgling city of Nairobi. *The Advertiser* had a report on 6 December 1907 about a consignment of sheep bought by Victor on behalf of Newland, Tarlton and Co. for Lord Delamere and other local landholders in British East Africa. These sheep came from both Anlaby, owned by Henry Dutton, and a property near Redhill in the Mid-North. They were transported from Port Adelaide to Durban and thence to Mombasa. More details about, 'N&T', as it became to be known, and its affairs follow later in this chapter.

The British had built a strategically placed railway, known by some as the 'Lunatic Line', from Mombasa on the east African coast, diagonally northwest to the southwestern shore of Lake Victoria, a distance of about fifty miles. The settlement of Nairobi was about halfway along this length of line. The British Government was keen to encourage ex-soldiers to take up selections along the railway line from Nairobi and to the northwest. It was here that Victor and Leslie Tarlton thought that they might settle on farms. Victor wrote to his mother in typically optimistic terms in February 1904 explaining that they and two other potential settlers were about to embark from South Africa on the SS *Africa* for Mombasa:

> You will be surprised to hear that though the poorest of the party (of four), I am the leader and quite an important person. You see I am the chronicler of the undertaking and as a result, the way is made very smooth for us. Of course, as settlers, we are only travelling 3rd class, but we have an eight-berth cabin to only four of us and are most comfortable. The Founder of the Settlement has given me the most flattering letters to the Administrator and has shown me the most confidential correspondence that has passed between him and the Foreign Office with the result that I am getting an insight into diplomatic service, such as I never hoped to come to me. I can tell you that I have such a brilliant second chance now as no man has a right to expect in his life.

Such comfort as Victor refers to seems to have been short-lived, as the following excerpt from his journal some time in the first half of 1904 shows. In his inimitable, beautifully written style, which says so much about this complex and extraordinarily sensitive and observant man, he wrote these astonishing words:

> I have just been aft, creeping in the shadow of deckhouses; slinking out of sight from stewards. There is ice aft – I have watched it, tinkling in long, bright glasses. There are pretty women there too – airy saloons and card-rooms, electrically fanned.
>
> I lie on my bunk writing this: many cockroaches are running races on the wooden walls and the seven similar bunks around me. This is the LOWER deck and there is no air or freshness

anywhere – only heat, moist human heat. On the bunk nearest to me a man is asleep, his shirt wide open at the neck and I can watch the sweat well up in great drops on his hairy chest and slowly trickle away. As for me? Well 'hot' is such an inadequate word; I hesitate to use it.

In the boarded hatchway outside, called by an enthusiastic Shipping Company – a 'pretty dining saloon', men of many nations are drinking beer, playing cards and talking at the tops of their voices. Somewhere a child is crying fretfully. On deck amongst windlasses, hen-coops, drying clothes and weary, close-penned horses, men are sleeping – stretched out on deck and hatch ... Presently, the saloon passengers will appear, carefree and well groomed. Then from behind our barriers we steerage 'trash' will watch them, appraising critically every well-turned neck or pretty arm. For ourselves, we are but barefoot, coatless creatures of another world.

Late into the night we shall sit, smoking and yarning – darting from women to eternity; from material ambitions back to women again, as man has ever done ... It is full of interest this steerage life up forward, comedy, tragedy and pathos; they are all around us ... this is life with the outside show all gone – life without privilege. One is always hearing new thoughts – the thoughts of people we never really meet under ordinary circumstances and for this alone, life is well worth living amongst this world's castaways ... Here are the tales of black, brown and white peoples – told frankly expecting neither praise nor judgement – such tales can never come to you unless you are actually sitting where they sit. There is misery and hardship – squalor – degradation, but there is also joy. It is the joy of knowing – knowing beyond further doubt, because you have actually lived, even if only for a short time, among the derelicts of many nations.

When they arrived at Mombasa on the east African coast, close to the equator, Victor noted that the local population was then a mixture of Portuguese, Turk, Arab, Moor and Persian, along with many native tribes. He refers to Mombasa as described as the 'Isle of Wars', with its history of carnage and bloodshed, also noting that at the time it was the most desirable harbour along that east coast. His party of four spent one night in Mombasa before boarding a small wood-fuelled train on the Lunatic Line for the highlands of East Africa. Victor's extraordinary journal describes this train trip as an unforgettable journey to Nairobi and beyond – their entry into a wonderland full of game animals and spectacular views. Nairobi was then a small galvanised-iron settlement, described by him as a 'blatant offence to nature'. From here, his party of now five white men and thirty 'native boys' went on to Lake Naivasha, sixty miles further northwest, where they had heard that land was available for selection. This lake is at an elevation of 6200 feet and, not surprisingly, the nights were very cold, despite this part of Africa being relatively close to the equator.

Victor and Leslie Tarlton had heard of land being available at Londiani, northwest of Nairobi. They set off on foot to find it, supported by a caravan of porters, described by Victor as 'the rawest of raw savages'. This march took them around the eastern slopes of an extinct volcano called Menengai, and Tarlton had the job of shooting game for meat. It was in this locality that they decided to apply for land, with Victor assigned to return to Nairobi by train to make their application. They were to be disappointed for, as it turned out, the land they sought had already been allocated. Nairobi in 1904 had basic government offices, a European hotel and a store, a Jewish produce dealer, a solicitor's office and a few Indian shops. The

Map of Kenya.
[Photo Nicholas Newland, 2015]

white population at that time was about one hundred officials and about a dozen settlers.

The actual genesis of Newland, Tarlton & Co or N&T is not clear. It is believed that it was established in 1904 as a general agency, taking on whatever work might come its way. An early role for the company was auctioning allotments in Nairobi, which seems to have been followed by a scheme of colonisation in British East Africa, called the 'Bowker Settlers'. It was colourfully described by Victor in his journal as: 'born of enthusiasm, insufficiently elaborated, poorly supported by the Government, and doomed to failure, including much heart-burning'.

Victor stayed in Nairobi to continue negotiations with the administrator. There was inevitable friction between the local government administrator and the scores of settlers, like Victor and Leslie Tarlton, who had come some distance to fulfil a dream, with the settlers indignant about their treatment and their perception of unreasonable protectorate laws. Interestingly, Victor was nominated as secretary of a settlers' association, working closely with a like-minded colonists' association. Negotiations between the administrator and these two associations culminated in better land-holding conditions, although Victor's stated dream of what he referred to as a 'model colony of farmers' was soon dispelled by what he saw and described as insuperable complications and sheer bureaucracy.

A likely effect of these complications was that, of the original party of four, two returned south, leaving Victor and Leslie Tarlton. The latter set off for five months with two companions on what Victor described as a poorly planned ivory shooting and trading expedition. During this time, Victor remained in Nairobi, befriended the local administration, became a member of the local club and developed N&T as a 'General Agency and

Auctioneering business'. He took on a range of business activities without the necessary experience and, when Leslie Tarlton returned, things were in a mess (Victor's words). He and Tarlton had considerable differences in expectations, with Victor in his journal noting that, 1904, which had begun 'with such bright hues of a dawning hope, ended in gloom and darkening with despondency and mutual dislike'.

However, both Victor and Leslie Tarlton recognised, among other things, an opportunity to cater for those who were seeking 'the African game experience', with Newland, Tarlton and Co. becoming the first to pioneer development of the safari business, in 1905. This part of the business became successful, with N&T attracting a wide range of luminaries, including English lords, dukes and marquises eager to partake of the safari experience. In Monty Brown's book *RJ*, published in 2004, Lord Cranworth, one of N&T's many clients, described Victor as 'about the hardest-working man I've known'.

Newland, Tarlton auction shed, Nairobi 1908.
[Photo courtesy Leonie Matheson]

Among these luminaries in 1909 was the recently retired Theodore Roosevelt, the twenty-sixth president of the United States of America, and his son Kermit, who together had an eleven-month safari, which included hunting big game. According to Victor's journal, Roosevelt was a lousy shot, being partially sight-impaired, although Kermit was somewhat better. Much of their shot game was sent to the fledgling Smithsonian Institution in Washington, DC, to become a principal part of the museum's collection of game animals from East Africa.

On safari with N&T in Kenya c. 1910.
[Photo courtesy Leonie Matheson]

Victor was conscious of the importance of local politics, being elected to the Nairobi Town Council, including a period as chairman. It is very likely that activities such as this were useful to him personally as well as to N&T in its attempts to become the preferred safari organisation in this part of East Africa. Victor clearly loved his East African life, although he also had a variety of memorable and testing experiences in the African bush, including becoming lost, suffering from sunstroke and going out for days shooting various species of game – purportedly for relaxation. He also seemed to be troubled by the influence Europeans inevitably were having on the local indigenous population. A paragraph from his journal indicates his reflections on being a white interloper among the locals and the lasting impact in East Africa of the white foreigner:

> I only am still awake; except for the stars, darkness now hides the wide open spaces around us. In a tiny circle of light I go once more over my exciting day. Then dimly aware that all around me dwell many strange people and many wild beasts, that after all it is their country, and that I am still the white intruder, I turn into my tent, and fall asleep.

He continues this theme further on:

> One night we camped on the borderland of the Lumbwa and Kavirondo tribes. Our camp was set near a number of stone-walled villages, then empty and overgrown. A mute and tragic testimony to past raids, massacres and swift retreats.

The N&T business continued to flourish during those years, a period when, according to Victor's journal, over seventy-five per cent of the shooting parties wanted N&T to organise and lead such parties. The great white hunter:

> had to have a strong character and be of tried personal integrity, besides being the possessor of much practical experience in big game hunting and have a wide knowledge of bushcraft. A 'White Hunter' was, therefore, no ordinary hunter trading in ivory, or a seeker after trophies. The 'White Hunter' was much more than an expert in seeking out and killing of game. He had to be able

> to organise, lead and maintain in the field parties of all kinds of untried people who wanted to go on 'safari' ... In the hands of the 'White Hunter' rested the care, safety, health and entertainment of these people ... A big Safari might take many months, and its fitting out and maintenance was quite a complicated matter. It could include many heavy trunks, much tentage, together with a dining tent, and a rich variety of food and drinks. There must be dependable guides, gun-bearers, cooks, and many porters or general bearers, and among these should be some adept in skinning and preserving skins. The whole personnel had to be well trained, for frequent erecting and breaking camp had to be done quickly and with military precision. A good Safari would include besides guns and ammunition – snowy-white table cloths and cocktail shakers.

Such an organiser was Victor, along with others such as the renowned white hunter R.J. Cunninghame, who worked for a time with N&T (see photograph page 171). Tarlton's health broke down in 1906, presumably from malaria or another fever, increasing the workload for Victor. He nevertheless took on the publication of a newspaper called the *Times of East Africa.* Brown's book *RJ*, on Cunninghame, uses an excerpt from Victor's journal in the front few pages, capturing well what life was like for him and his associates:

> Until dark we sit, smoke and yarn – we three white men. One is a pallid wreck slowly recovering from a bout of fever; and one has bright eyes and headache – sure signals of an approaching attack. I am still just a wandering mortal who listens wistfully to their talk ... But one cannot help wondering what manner of men these will be then this tropic sun has done with them. For that matter, what will become of us all in our old age, with Africa's cursed

fever in our veins, and Africa's claws still holding us captive by its strange seductions?

These very well-chosen words, which encompass eloquently the allure of East Africa – and its not-so-pleasant side effects – to non-indigenous people, illustrate Victor's introspection and his capacity to reflect profoundly on his circumstances.

In June 1907, according to Bulbeck's biographical account, Victor received a telegram from Adelaide, which contained the following words: 'Please come to me at once'. It is not entirely clear who the author was, but it is reasonable to assume it was from his ideal girl Elsie Porter, his wife-to-be. We do know however that he married Elsie on 20 April 1909 and took her back to Nairobi, where he had to begin preparations for the Roosevelt safari.

Victor's involvement in local politics led, in 1910, to his being nominated to the British East Africa colony's Legislative Council.

Victor Newland's wedding party 1909; from left, F.W. Porter & wife, Victor and Elsie, on far right Jane Newland (sitting) and Simpson (standing).
[Photo courtesy Leonie Matheson]

Despite all that Victor had experienced to this point, his adventures continued. He wrote to his parents while on a trip to England in 1911, during which he, his wife, nurse and young daughters all survived a shipwreck somewhere off the French coast. The following edited version of his letter shows it must have been an exceptionally trying time for them all:

> Gibraltar
> 18/12/11
> My dear Father and Mother,
>
> I hope you have not been having too exciting a time over our unpleasant experience on the 'Delhi', but I sent a wireless to Mr Porter [Victor's father-in-law] as soon as possible after we struck saying that we were safe and no doubt he passed the news on to you. Now that it is all over, I can see that the position was more terrifying than actually dangerous whilst we were on board, but at the time all we knew was that we were on a ship wrecked vessel being pounded on the shore by waves which frequently swept funnel high and there was mighty little feeling of safety amongst us. It was about 1 o'clock when we grounded and Elsie and I were forgotten, having changed our cabin. We were at last called by the deck steward just as we realised from the awful bumping that some disaster had happened. Ten minutes after we got on deck our cabin was being battered by huge seas as the vessel listed and every boat on that side of the ship was smashed to smithereens ... It was nerve-racking work waiting for dawn with the vessel being lifted and smashed down again every few minutes and blinding squalls of rain shutting out land and everything else at intervals. Daylight came about 7 o'clock and we found ourselves about 300 yards from a sandy beach, between which and ourselves huge surfs were breaking. No

attempt at rescue was made until the arrival of a French cruiser from Tangiers or Gibraltar about 9 o'clock. Her crew showed marvellous pluck, putting off a small steam pinnace, which had a tremendous fight getting alongside. Later on, British war boats and salvage steamers arrived but did nothing beyond standing by to begin with and meanwhile the children with one or two women were embarked on the French pinnace, Margaret amongst them, there being no room for Elsie or nurse who were put in one of the ship's lifeboats and towed off by the pinnace … It was an awful experience watching that little French pinnace fighting the surf with most of our womenfolk depending on her and when the towline broke at the most critical point of all, we were nearly heartbroken … On board the ship, we felt much happier when the women were in safety, but it was pretty rotten all day watching boat after boat smashed up landing people or being capsized in the surf before reaching shore … I did not get off until the following day, being left behind with 11 other passengers, but we did not have a bad night, though all lights failed and about 4 am an extra big sea slewed us round a bit, and the fore bulkhead went and all sorts of grinding noises made one think for a bit that the vessel was breaking up however, we were all tired out and got a pretty good night's rest. Next day a rocket apparatus was at work onshore and after about a dozen attempts a line reached us and soon we were all hard at work hauling a stout rope ashore. This was fixed to the foretop and after an early lunch we climbed the mast in turn, struggled in to a life belt attached to a pully [sic], with our legs through a kind of breeches arrangement and went flying through the air to the surf – I had quite an enjoyable passage, did not get a mouthful of water and landed with a dry box of matches in my hat, which I had securely tied on … I will write again by next mail and meanwhile am cabling Mr Porter

as soon as our movements are decided upon, he having sent us a reply paid wire to enable us to keep in touch. Love to you all from us all.
Yr affec son
VMNewland

Victor took his family back to Nairobi, and the three years leading up to the First World War appear to have been largely without the sorts of dramatic incidents that had been part of his life as a single man. Over these years, both the colonies of British East Africa and German East Africa had continued to develop and attract investment. The safari business and other N&T ventures also flourished. However, as the conflict with Germany intensified, leading ultimately to the First World War, Victor's sense of responsibility to his family meant that, although they were all in South Australia at the time, he had no hesitation in returning to Nairobi alone. He sought to enlist and fight, despite by then being over twenty-eight years old. Since he was regarded by Army authorities as too old to fight, he joined the East Africa Transport Corps as a lieutenant, being promoted to major in late 1915.

The first page of a letter written by Victor on Newland, Tarlton & Co. letterhead to Colonel Roosevelt makes for interesting reading and is included below. Apart from the letter's discussion of the safari business, it shows the sort of environment in which he found himself prior to enlisting in British East Africa and joining the British Army. It also shows how N&T communicated with future, present and past clients:

Typically reflecting his patriotic values, Victor wrote to his father on 2 November 1915 stating that:

I noticed in a letter received from you last week a reference to some remark I made about my war losses – I hope I did not

> grumble, for my real belief is that no sacrifice we younger men can make is too great, if by making it, we can end this horrible war.

Notwithstanding his views about the war in East Africa, Victor's experience and his age meant that he saw little fighting. Given the knowledge and the experience gained from running N&T, he became involved in arranging supplies to the various fighting forces, despite the proximity of German East Africa (subsequently Tanganyika and now Tanzania), just over the northwest border of British East Africa. His deployment here by Army authorities did not worry Victor duly, given his desire for adventure, and keeping fighting troops appropriately supplied was an essential activity. His services were well appreciated and he was awarded the Military Cross in 1917 and the Order of the British Empire (OBE) in 1919.

This posting nevertheless was arduous, and was physically as well as personally very demanding. On 13 May 1918, Victor wrote the following to his father:

> You will be pleased to learn that I have made a reputation in Portuguese East Africa, but the strain has been simply appalling as we have been up against conditions which I can only describe to you in person. On top of military conditions, I have had malaria, rheumatism, neuralgia, abscess of the jaw and an injury to one's eye, which not only caused me agony, but still affects the sight, though this is only temporary – I am glad to say however that I have not yet been off duty a whole day and really believe I can see the thing thru – how tired I am of it all is beyond words.

The excerpt below was written in February 1919 when Victor and his family were returning from East Africa to South Australia via Melbourne. As noted earlier, it confirms my opinion that Victor suffered more from his war and other near-death experiences and his subsequent difficulties as a settler in British East Africa (now known as Kenya) than perhaps he was prepared to admit:

> We spent yesterday (Sunday) out with the MacMeikans and the quiet day did us both good – Lizzie [née Waite] and her husband were both awfully good to us and for the first time since I finished up soldiering I felt normal. My nerves have been all to pieces for a long time and I have hated being cooped up in a ship with a crowd of people – Hotels are not much better and it is a tremendous relief to get amongst friends again.

Victor returned to British East Africa some time in mid-1919, since at that stage it was still home for his family. On his way back, he received a letter from Leslie Tarlton in Durban, South Africa, about which he wrote in the following terms to his parents:

> A long business letter from Tarlton has pretty much destroyed any enjoyment I might have got out of Durban, he having written to say that he has left Newland Tarlton & Co. to go on the land, merely remaining an ordinary director of the Co. The Co's. affairs have been amalgamated on lines that do not suit me at all and though a managing directorship has been reserved for me at a salary of 1,200 pounds a year ... things will have to be altered to suit my ideas before I will bind myself to the Company. The business has expanded enormously and is working on a 40,000 pound overdraft which makes me shiver to think of.

According to Bulbeck's account, N&T suffered the effects of the post-war financial depression and ceased providing safaris as N&T, although the company name continues to survive. Victor withdrew from the company, although Leslie Tarlton continued to operate, but under the different company name of Safariland Ltd. Victor and his family finally returned to Australia in 1923. In that year, apparently with the help of his father-in-law F.W. Porter, who was a successful stockbroker, he bought a seat on the Adelaide Stock Exchange and in 1926 entered into a partnership with R.C. Hunter, the partnership being named Newland, Hunter and Co.

Victor's interest in politics continued, with his election in 1933 to the seat of North Adelaide in the South Australian House of Assembly. The book *Bulls Bears and Wildcats* by R.M. Gibbs (Peacock Publications, 1988) recounts that in 1935 Victor opposed a measure to increase parliamentarians' salaries; they had been reduced during the Great Depression. He was accused by some of his political colleagues of having an alternative source of income, that is, from his involvement with the stock exchange. In the history of politics, such opposition to a salary increase must indeed be rare.

He and Elsie went to Europe in 1938 and on his return to South Australia, Victor offered his services to the Second World War effort, although by then he was over sixty. After the war, Newland, Hunter and Co. was reconstituted, albeit briefly and unsuccessfully. His wife Elsie died in 1950.

Victor died on 14 January 1953, and Bulbeck's account describes a moving incident that occurred at his funeral, which may well be a reflection of his impact on others during his life:

> The funeral was not without its incident. As the flag-draped coffin, bearing V.M. Newland's decorations and medals left the house, there stood at the gate an unknown, shabby old man. He was wearing his Boer War medals, with tears running down his careworn face, he came to attention, saluted as the coffin passed

and then turned and shuffled away. So the unknown had come to see that an old comrade should not pass on his way unnoticed by the old brigade.

The following was kindly written for this book by Leonie Matheson, whose mother was Margaret Newland, Victor's younger daughter, who supplied most of the material about Victor that appears in this book. She wrote the following excerpt in 2014 about her grandfather at my request, which I include verbatim:

Simpson Newland was small in stature. Some small people have a tough side to them, and when my grandfather had enlisted to go to the Boer War he was sent off with this from his father : 'I do not expect you to win the VC but if you are a coward don't come home'.

If this was a challenge to VMN he certainly responded to it in his role as a soldier in South Africa and later in British East Africa, as an early settler in Kenya where he was an auctioneer, later as Chair of the Nairobi Town Council and then as a member for four years of the Legislative Council, as President of the Associated Chambers of Commerce and as founder of the safari firm Newland and Tarlton with his friend Leslie Tarlton. His exhausting years in Africa and the fevers they produced took their toll, forcing him and his family back to Adelaide.

I knew him well when my mother and I lived with him at Lexden [a house in Molesworth St, North Adelaide] during the war years. His imagination delighted a young girl with his stories of his African adventures, but the lion's head he kept in his small library with its piercing eyes terrified me, and to think that he shot it! Grandfather and I had wonderful adventures scrambling up the creek at Undelcarra in Burnside where he and his brothers had played Cowboys and Indians. Further over the paddocks lived Effie Ferguson, a fascinating old lady with white hair in a bun and a cameo brooch on a black velvet ribbon around her neck. She had given him a gold pencil, which he took to the Boer War.

We did the weekly shopping together in his Morris car and he talked football to me. He had the No 1 ticket for Prospect [now North Adelaide Football Club]. There were no Easter eggs then but the ' lucky star' appeared in the sky. It had left African silver coins at various points around the garden path for me to find. I still have them on a silver necklace. I was so sad later that he contracted Parkinson's Disease which disabled him. All he wanted was to have one last trip to his beloved Kenya.'

Mention has already been made of Victor's association with Harry 'the Breaker' Morant. Morant's life and death were the subject of a film *Breaker Morant*, made about thirty years ago by director Bruce Beresford, starring English actor Edward Woodward in the role of the Breaker and Australian actor Jack Thompson as Morant's defence lawyer. It was filmed at Burra in South Australia's Mid-North. A tribute to Morant was written some time in 1901 by Victor, who apparently was present at his execution by a British Army firing squad. It is written in a style that reflects those Edwardian times and, to my mind, says as much about Victor as it does about Morant. It has been included in its entirety both because it is extremely well written and also because it provides an interesting historical record. It is a fitting conclusion to the chapter on a man who can only be described as extraordinary and who lived a remarkable life.

Major VM Newland's tribute to Harry 'Breaker' Morant dec.d.

Have you ever known the grim, chill dawn in a South African winter, when rifle and stirrup are mates in their coldness, and with crackling rime under your horse's hoofs? That is misery, grey, cheerless misery; but, beyond it, lies the hope of the noonday sun. Have you heard rifles snarl, and bullets spit curses while your well-loved guns are bogged in spruit or donga? That is misery too; but amidst the plunging horses, shouting drivers, dying comrades is honour to be won, and, if death come, it is great in its suddenness.

It is bitter, cruelly bitter, when a man's nerve fails in a hot rush on a position, but honour returns with a setting of teeth and a surge of pride that lifts him, a trembling creature and drives him on again, a warrior.

In these moments, England's ne'er-do-wells achieve, perhaps in the grip of death itself, a ripe honour that all life else has denied – self passes: the pride of Homeland lives – a moment's fighting, grim and silent: or cursing, dinful – a crash of dropped rifle on rock, the work of a fallen body, and the wickedness of wanton years dies with a praising breath: we remember the berserk valour and forget the sin.

But there are black sheep who outlive the moment's glory to sin again and to outlive their new won honour: perchance to die a felon's death, where there is no redemption, save in the manner of dying.

'The Breaker' – poor beggar, how well I remember him, outcast, boon comrade, drunken beast, and brave man. It seems but yesterday we trekked, starved, stole, and fought together – what a sot he was in towns – what a mate in those hours of night watch or day march, what tales he could tell, what merry rhymes recite.

And there were days before, too, days down in great sunny Australia, days of racing, begging and starving, days of wine and women, rags, drunkenness and disgrace – poor old Breaker! Fearless of offence or foe, on principle ne'er paying a debt, to women as courteous as a knight of chivalry, now swaggie, now

> gentleman rider, now cadger, now fleeing the clutches of a stern, unpoetical law – in the last phase of all; a commissioned officer, he took men's God-given lives, slew surrendered foes, so came court-martial, lagging days, a firing party and death.
>
> I can see it all so plainly even yet: his grotesque bad face with its redeeming smile of manhood; his debonair swagger out into the damp coolness of morning: his bright greeting to all.
>
> God: how dreadful it was when they bound his eyes and sat him in the chair, square and fearless, a dead man yet alive.
>
> 'Ready!' My knees are weak as I write the word – 'Present!' An order tremulous – the Officer-in Charge, grey-faced, unnerved, and, watching, I see his throat rise in great gulps, his lips quiver. There is a silence of seconds that are hours in their intensity. Then from the chair rises the Breaker; down flutters the blinding kerchief: I catch a glimpse of tawny, fearless eyes alight with understanding and pity for the man who must call death upon him.
>
> Lightly he swings his hand to his breast: 'There, boys', he says, 'don't miss.' Smartly he drops his hands to his sides – square set his shoulders: a steady, motionless figure he stands: and clear, stern and painful comes the word of his doom – 'Fire!'

Victor was undoubtedly someone very special. Victor's life, as much as has been recounted here and despite its being somewhat abridged, is one that combines huge amounts of drama, excitement and risk taking, with humility, decency, honour and other 'manly' characteristics. His parents surely could not have been anything but proud that so many outstanding achievements could be fitted into the life of one of their sons.

8

Clive Newland

BORN 14 SEPTEMBER 1878, DIED 25 JANUARY 1919

The history and circumstances of the two youngest brothers are more obscure, since, as we know, records of their activities are relatively scant compared with their older brothers. It is unfortunate that what is now most known about Clive is connected to the dreadful circumstances of his premature death, rather than from the achievements of his relatively short life, of about forty years. Building a picture of Clive has, by comparison with some of his brothers, been somewhat difficult. However, correspondence from Henry to his father in early 1919 after Clive's mortal accident, described below, refers to Clive as 'the apple of his parents' eyes'. Given the deeds of his other brothers, this is praise indeed.

Although the circumstances of Clive's early boyhood life are not spelled out, it is likely, as with his brothers, that his father expected him to 'shape up' and not to shirk his responsibilities. In the excerpt from a letter to his eldest son Henry on 20 December 1897 – largely concerning Clive's performance in exams – Simpson makes his fatherly expectations quite clear:

> You will be sorry as we all were to hear that Clive did not pass. I certainly cannot blame him for not working. Work hard he undoubtedly did and the disappointment has been keen for him. Mathematics pulled him down and in that subject I have always heard he is not strong. At present I have not decided if he is to go on in the A or B course but considering his youth and that I do not like a son of mine to give up anything once begun I shall probably let him try again.

As with Victor and Ralph, Clive appears to have been a keen horseman. The following extract from one of his father's letters, dated 5 June 1901 and again to son Henry, is surprising, in that he makes it clear that hunting is not a sport he believed Clive should take up. From what we know of Simpson, we would expect him to consider hunting to be a 'manly' pursuit:

> I am sorry to say Clive has bought a hunter as a bad fall would probably mean the loss of a year but he was advised by Dr Marten to give up lacrosse because of his knee infection & he says 'a fellow must do something' & I must admit the necessity of that where young blood is concerned. Still I think he might have left hunting alone.

Similar to his brothers, Clive was an imposing, albeit relatively small, figure, in the manner of his father. He seemed to want to be viewed as an achiever, an aspiration that in all probability he saw in his brothers and certainly in his father. In the many letters written from Africa by his older brother Victor (by three years), Clive is mentioned several times, mostly in relation to his studies and exams; he wanted to follow in eldest brother Henry's footsteps to become some sort of medical practitioner, although his parents seemed unsure of whether he had the intellectual and mental capacity to become a doctor. In the end Clive did take up medicine, also emulating Henry in furthering his medical studies in London. It appears that, during his time there, the two brothers became quite close, as is recounted below. Surprisingly, however, little mention is made of Clive in Henry's quite extensive letters to his parents over a decade or more.

Clive's love of sport brought him into regular contact with his older brother Philip, who seemed to be regarded as 'the sportsman' of the family, despite all of the brothers demonstrating sporting ability and interest. Although Philip appeared to be the most gifted sportsman, Clive too was apparently keen on lacrosse, along with his younger brother Ralph. It was as if this was part of what was expected of them.

Clive Newland c. 1900.

Simpson in his *Memoirs* refers to two sons Philip and Clive without mentioning their names when he says: 'Five sons were born to us; two are tragically dead … '

Ralph was still alive when Simpson wrote those words. Having his eldest brother Henry as a successful surgeon and his elder brother Philip, among other things, a highly competent sportsman would have been something of a test for Clive. Brother Victor was in Africa at this time, living a dangerous life. Clive however was prepared to take up his own challenge, following brother Henry to London after completing his medical training in Adelaide. In one of the few letters in the State Library of South Australia's collection, Clive wrote to his father on 12 March 1903 in the following terms, seeking financial help:

> I am sure that any little hardship at the beginning with me asked to work up the ladder gradually at the commencement would make the later and more successful life all the more enjoyable. I must say that I do not like asking you for this favour for you have already been so good to me and done so much …

In the same year, Lizzie Waite, who was a good family friend, and with Victor in particular, visited London, and Clive showed her around the hospital where he had held a position for some months as Ophthalmic Clinical Assistant. He mentions in correspondence with his father, with whom he had a very close relationship, that he was keen to be a country doctor on his return to South Australia. Country doctors must be willing to try their skill at most things and Clive appears to be no exception: 'I've seen such a lot of operating since I arrived that I am keen to tackle anything provided I can get an assistant to help'.

Clive's appalling death was an enormous blow to his wife Marjorie (née Hamilton) and to his parents and brothers. Letters in the State Library, excerpts of which are below, describe their anguish. The first excerpt is from Marjorie to Clive's father Simpson, dated 5 February 1919, written from Clive and Marjorie's house Colmore, which still stands on Doctor's Road, Morphett Vale, in South Australia: 'You have been so much in my thoughts for I know he was the dearest of all your sons to you just as he was the dearest of all the world to me'.

On the same day, Simpson wrote to Henry in London reflecting his great anguish and grief:

> His fate is such a diabolically cruel one that every fibre and feeling in me revolts at it. I am assured that 'all things work together for good' ultimately but that is surely about the bitterest lie ever written.

In his response to his mother that day from Queen's Hospital, London, Henry wrote to his mother:

> It was a terrible shock to hear by cable on Friday that Clive had been killed on the railway he had done so much to obtain for his district. I have the deepest feeling for you and the Pater in your distress. Poor old Pater, Clive was the apple of his eye and the blow is the sorest possible because so inconceivable. Clive and Marjorie were so devoted to one another and he was such a loving husband to her that her world will be dark and lonely indeed.

Another of Henry's letters to his father, written some months later, on 3 October 1919, expressing sympathy for Clive's death, again describes Clive as 'the apple of his eye'. One wonders what the future might have held for them if both Philip and Clive had lived for another thirty years. The circumstances of Clive's premature death could scarcely be more horrifying and it is little wonder that his parents and siblings reacted in the way that they did.

The following text has kindly been provided to me by Clive's granddaughter Helena Tonkin (née Newland). Helena has three brothers, all of whom are interested in their paternal grandfather. Yet none of them knows much about Clive, except the horrific circumstances of his relatively short life, his death tragically depriving his family, parents, brothers and friends of a loved one. Helena's contribution to this book reveals something of Clive's character and motivation, which could not easily been gleaned in other ways, particularly the second to fourth paragraphs:

> Tragically my grandfather was killed in an accident on Saturday, January 25th 1919, just three years after his parents had buried his older brother Philip. Both these men were only 41 years of age. Clive's death had huge ramifications for his young family living south of Adelaide in Morphett Vale, turning their lives upside down.
>
> Clive was born into the Newland household on September 14th, 1878. Perhaps his parents, Simpson and Jane, had thoughts of a daughter during this pregnancy [I understand that this may indeed have been the case, with the name Sophie even chosen in anticipation], but it was not to be and they named their fourth son Clive. Although he was the fourth son in the family he had two 'firsts'. He was the first baby to be born at Undelcarra, the newly acquired home in the suburb of Burnside, and he was the first married. Simpson and Jane moved from Marra on the Darling River with their three boys prior to Clive's birth. The stately two-storey home was surrounded by large grounds and included a coachman's cottage, an orchard, a horse and cattle paddock, a creek and dams to provide water, all of which provided freedom

and space. He spent his childhood romping in this paradise for boys. When Clive was ready for school he followed his brothers attending Queen's and St. Peters College. From an early age he showed great promise and had inherited many traits of his revered father, including a studious temperament.

Clive shared interests with his eldest brothers, his career with Henry and sport with Philip. Henry, five years his senior had chosen a career in Medicine and so did Clive, the former becoming a surgeon while Clive became a general practitioner. He gained his M.B. at Adelaide University and his M.R.C.S and L.R.C.P. diplomas at the London University. Philip and Clive played Lacrosse at the highest level and he loved cricket. Clive had an engaging personality and made friends easily from an early age.

One of his friends was George Jones who he met at Queen's School. When they left the school they swapped mementos for good luck and tokens of their friendship. Clive gave George a miniature spinning wooden top, one inch high. George became an explorer and lost his life in the desert in Western Australia in 1896 whilst a member of the ill-fated Calvert Expedition. Amazingly the top was found knotted into the corner of a handkerchief on his body. Some reports suggested that while aborigines took his clothing, they left the top thinking it may be some special little god token. Eventually this tiny top made its way back to Clive and I have it today. George had given his friend a miniature cricket ball which Clive carried about in his pocket.

Henry and Clive enjoyed a very close friendship throughout Clive's short life. They had much in common and there was a strong family resemblance. Clive had a leaner build, neither were tall men and both wore their hair short, parted and neatly combed across strong foreheads. Henry had a softer more gentle

Clive Newland's wedding party in 1903. His brother Henry is best man.
[Photo courtesy Mrs Helena Tonkin]

countenance than Clive who was more angular and displaying the aloof demeanour of the times.

Clive married Marjorie Hamilton in the spring of 1903 and was the first of the boys to marry. Henry was the best man and three flower girls completed the small bridal party. The bride with tulle and flowers, men resplendent in their morning suits.

Clive was now a qualified General Practitioner and they made their home in Morphett Vale where he was the local Doctor. Morphett Vale was a rural hamlet thirty kilometres south of Adelaide and one of the earliest settlements outside of Adelaide, rich with pioneering history. In 1853 the first meeting of the District Council was held there, wells were sunk and wattle and bark dwellings erected using oxen to haul wooden logs. The mail coach left promptly at 8 a.m. every Saturday morning, and locals would set their watches by it. As time passed, bluestone from the local quarry and slate from Willunga were used to build more substantial cottages and houses, and it was in one of these, 'Colmore', that Clive and his family lived. Clive was the fourth doctor to live in the shady two-level home which still stands today albeit minus its verandah. It is nestled back from the corner on the main road from Adelaide to Victor Harbor and Doctor's Road. In this semi-rural setting Clive and Marjorie raised three boys in relative isolation, Clive attended his patients, scampering to their homes on his motorbike.

Three boys were born while they lived at 'Colmore', Clive Thomas, Rupert and James Hamilton. The children all had serious health problems. James, the youngest was born with pyloric stenosis, a thickening of the muscle where the stomach joins the small intestine which induced frequent and severe vomiting. Henry operated on him in one of the first surgical procedures of its kind in the state. Henry saved his life. Middle son Rupert was afflicted with epilepsy. His life was certainly diminished as a result and his seizures were severe requiring him to be restrained. He drowned when swimming when he was 22 years old.

Tom (as the eldest son was called) lost his left eye in an accident in the garden at home. The muscles of the eye caused much trouble and it was difficult keeping a glass eye in place. Tom had a wicked sense of humour and enjoyed terrifying people by popping out the glass eye. In later life the eye muscle weakened so much he gave up the glass eye and wore a patch which he wore with great style and panache!

The following report of Clive's death appeared in the *Adelaide Advertiser* on 25 January 1919.

Railway Accidents

Dr. Clive Newland Killed.

A fatal accident occurred to Dr. Clive Newland of Morphett Vale, on January 25, while he was answering, on his motor cycle, an urgent call to Noarlunga. No one actually witnessed the accident, which happened on the railway line, near Morphett Vale, about 11 a.m. It appears from what can be gathered from those who arrived on the scene shortly afterwards, among whom was Mr Philip R. Lee, of Grant-avenue, Toorak, that it was connected with the passing of the 9.7 mixed from Adelaide about ten minutes before Mr Lee reached the spot. The first people at the crossing, which is about two miles and a quarter from Morphett Vale, were an elderly gentleman, two ladies, and their chauffeur, in a motor car. It was impossible to see anything of the unfortunate victim until the motor was almost on top of him. The chauffeur immediately went to the house nearby for assistance, but there was only a lady there. When he returned, Mr Lee, who was motoring home from Victor Harbor, arrived. About the same time, a motor car with four gentlemen passengers reached the spot. The men got the Doctor into Mr. Lee's car and Mr Lee brought him straight to Parkwynd Hospital, Wakefield-street. Mr Lee stated that it appeared to him the doctor had been riding his motor cycle against a strong head wind, and must have had his head down, so that he failed to notice the oncoming train, until it was almost upon him. He then evidently swerved sharply in an attempt to get out of the way over the crossing cattle-pit. When he was first observed he was lying in a heap with his limbs doubled up under him, and was in a terrible state. The barbed wire of the cattle-pit was carried ten or twelve yards away, and

Mr Lee surmises that the doctor must have been hit by one of the carriages of the train. It was about 1 o'clock when the sufferer reached the hospital, and Drs Poulton, Ray, Scott, and Marten were there to attend to him. It was found that both his legs were broken, that he was suffering from serious skull injuries, and that he had been otherwise hurt. His condition was regarded as critical, and it was impossible to do much to relieve the sufferer, owing to the serious condition. Mr Simpson Newland, his father, and Mrs Newland were at Victor Harbor, and a message was sent to them to come to the city at once. The doctor's wife was also summoned to the city. The patient remained unconscious, and died shortly before 6 o'clock.

The railway authorities in Adelaide have not received any report of the occurrence from the officials who were on the train, and telephone enquiries by the secretary to the Railways Commissioner supported the view that the engine-driver and guard were unaware an accident had happened.

The Coroner did not consider an inquest necessary.

Dr Newland was the fourth son of Mr. Simpson Newland. He was born at 'Undelcarra,' Burnside, in 1879, [actually 1878] and attended Queen's School and St. Peter's College. At an early age he gave promise of great attainments. Bearing a name honored in the community because of his father's splendid service rendered as a pioneer, publicist and path finder, the son of the distinguished author of 'Paving the Way,' possessed many of the qualities which were so conspicuous in his sire. He took his M.B. degree at the Adelaide University, and his M.R.C.S. and L.R.C.P. diplomas at the London University. Throughout his course he displayed marked natural ability, and the power of application which indicate the student temperament. By his genial disposition he made many friends, and although an earnest worker he found time for recreation in the field of sport. He was a man of versatile sympathies, both in his University days and in after life.

On his return to Adelaide 15 years ago he married Marjorie, daughter of the late Dr. A.A. Hamilton, and immediately began practice at Morphett Vale, where his many fine qualities found speedy recognition, in the high esteem in which he was held. Dr Newland in his college days was a fine lacrosse player, and was always interested in cricket. After he took up his residence at Morphett Vale he gave a considerable amount of his time to public affairs, especially in connection with agricultural and horticultural pursuits. At the time of his death he was president of the Morphett Vale Agricultural Society, which owed much to his enthusiasm. His death will be a great loss to the district, in which he was a familiar figure. He leaves a widow and three sons, the eldest of which is about 13 years of age.

Helena Tonkin continues:

Marjorie was left bereft with three young boys in a small rural hamlet without a future. She was forced to move back to the city, where she and Clive were brought up and purchased a charming Victorian bluestone residence in Strangways Terrace, North Adelaide, just up the road from Henry who became the children's guardian. We called him Uncle Hal and he was often called to discipline the spirited boys and kept a watchful eye. He became a surrogate father and grandfather to our family and would often walk down the back lane from Ward Street to visit our grandmother, or pop in on his way to the Adelaide Oval. I remember his humble presence, his erect proud stance, his bow ties and his deafness; a man who had touched so many lives in

> his brilliant career. My father often said he wanted to outlive Uncle Hal's 96 years, this was some sort of challenge but Dad succumbed six years short of the mark.

Undoubtedly more information on Clive would have been welcome. Because there is so little, what we do have becomes all the more important, adding further depth to the portrait of these five men, the remarkable sons of Simpson and Jane Newland.

9

Ralph Dimock Newland

BORN 16 MARCH 1880, DIED 20 SEPTEMBER 1933

Born in 1880, my grandfather Ralph was the youngest of Simpson and Jane's sons. He also died relatively young, at fifty-three, in 1933. The reasons for his premature death are not entirely clear, although it is understood that his health may well have been affected by his work as a mining or chemical engineer in the South African gold mines early in the twentieth century. Once again, details are scant, although it is understood that gold-mining techniques early in the twentieth century were not generally conducive to good health.

Ralph was unwell for many years, apparently becoming extremely ill at the age of forty-six. For the following seven years, up to his death, he was something of an invalid. As mentioned at the beginning of this history, his gravestone and some family records have his second name spelt with a double 'm': 'Dimmock' as distinct from Dimock, as shown on his birth and death certificates. Whether his parents recorded his name incorrectly at his birth is a matter of conjecture. A study of family records shows clearly that 'Dimmock' was the surname of his great grandparents.

Much of what is recounted in this chapter comes largely from letters from his two elder brothers, who were regular correspondents with their parents and others. It is likely that Ralph was also, although no records exist to confirm this. Similar to the situation of Clive, Ralph's descendants know little more about him than is contained in this chapter. Unfortunately, even less is known about Ralph than Clive, notwithstanding his longer life.

Ralph's boyhood life at Undelcarra was undoubtedly similar to his siblings, raised in circumstances largely reserved for the well-off. From the correspondence that exists, he was apparently a fine horseman and, as with his brothers, was a keen sportsman, particularly excelling in athletics, lacrosse and cricket. To that extent, he followed in his brother Philip's footsteps, as the photograph of the lacrosse team earlier indicates. Ralph's education mirrored that of his brothers; he started primary education at Queen's School and moved to St Peter's College for his secondary education.

My family has a trophy for the half-mile running race won by Ralph as a sixteen-year-old, in 1896, when at St Peter's College. Also, while there is no clear evidence that religion was important to him, I have in my possession a beautiful leather-bound copy of a bible containing maps of the Peninsula of Sinai, Canaan and its tribes, Palestine, a route map of the Apostle Paul, Jerusalem and Assyria. In the front is a simple message which indicates something of the relationship between his mother and her youngest son: 'To my dear Ralph with his Mother's love. Undelcarra, January 12th 1903'. Ralph would have been just under twenty-three years old at that time, having graduated from the Adelaide School of Mines in 1902.

The family also has Ralph's photograph album, begun by him in1904, although unfortunately many of the photographs are not dated or labelled. Several of these photos were taken at Undelcarra and show that life must have been good and comfortable, notwithstanding Simpson's efforts in making his sons tough, self-reliant and appreciative of their fortunate circumstances. Among these photographs is one of Ralph himself, shown below, sitting outside the front door of the neighbouring Ferguson house, Chiverton. There is a clear family resemblance and, like his brothers, he was a good-looking man.

Other pictures taken at Chiverton are included in the album.

Ralph Dimock Newland c. 1901.
[Photo Newland Family Archives]

My cousin Leonie Matheson reported that as a young man Ralph embarked upon a sailing trip with his good friend Harry Dutton, but there are no photographs of this. They sailed from Port Victor to Kangaroo Island, a journey along an unforgiving coastline that had claimed its share of ships, and then across the treacherous Backstairs Passage, with its surging currents. This was no mean feat and certainly not a sailing journey for the faint-hearted.

Other photographs depict various interstate lacrosse teams and matches in progress, in which brother Philip is also shown, invariably as captain. Ralph was also a member of the Iroquois Lacrosse Club, as is shown in a stand-alone photograph of the team taken in 1898 and now in my possession. He played lacrosse at state level around this time as part of the South Australian team, but again details are sketchy.

A considerable number of the pictures in the photo album were taken in South Africa and demonstrate his interest in mining matters during the time he spent there. Other photos show his brother Philip dressed to play lacrosse, Victor in uniform on his horse as he prepared to depart for the Boer War in 1899, and his father attempting, not with obvious success, to swing a golf club. The album also contains photographs taken in 1901 at Wallaroo mine in South Australia, as well as in other parts of the world, including New Zealand and Ceylon (as it was then), to which Ralph travelled in 1915 after the premature death of his first wife Hazel. A page is devoted to Christmas greetings for 1903 and is made up of eight humorous, less than politically correct, drawings picturing 'blackboys' wielding spears, including one of a white person being dragged to a cooking pot, with the fire being tended by a 'blackboy'. This page is labelled 'Nourse Deep Gold Mine Johannesburg South Africa'. These drawings are quite well executed and clearly done by Ralph as the compiler of the album. They show some artistic skill on his part. My father and two of my sisters certainly had artistic skill, which may in part have been inherited from Ralph.

Whether Ralph enjoyed life while in South Africa is unknown, although the following excerpt from a letter written by Victor on 1 May 1900 from Karee's Kloof in South Africa suggests that this is the case and that Ralph probably had a good sense of humour:

> Ralph has written me a most amusing letter. If ever a chap is happy he is – with his horseriding, many friends and Hazel. He has asked me for a battlefield curio for her – they are easy enough to get.

The photos of Ralph himself in the 1904 album, one of which is included in this chapter, show an apparently quiet, purposeful and serious man, but perhaps a bit aloof. If these photos are any indication, his time in the South African gold mines as a chemical engineer was one where work was taken seriously, with several of the photos of a technical nature, showing mining infrastructure. Yet there was also time for fishing, swimming and cricket, while a letter penned by Victor from Esterfabruken confirms Ralph's pleasure in horseriding: 'What a jolly good thing it is Ralph becoming such an enthusiastic horseman'. We know from the letters his brother Victor wrote to their parents that Ralph made the most of his South African sojourn. There are also photos of indigenous Africans, which, had they been labelled, might have told more about his subjects, as well as about him and his activities at the time. It can be but presumed that such photos were taken and/or included for some reason.

Victor's many letters from Africa to his parents occasionally reveal snippets of information about Ralph. On 14 February 1903, Victor wrote to his mother: 'I spent a night out at the mine with Ralph last week and enjoyed a yarn with him over things in general'.

Eight months later, he says in another letter to his parents: 'I have not seen Ralph for a long time but hear continued good reports of him ...' Two weeks after this date, on 30 October 1903, Victor reports as follows: 'Ralph has developed a double chin as a result of his healthy, happy life and when I saw him last week, he was as keen as ever'.

Ralph suffered the misfortune of his wife Hazel's early death on 4 November 1915; she was aged just twenty-eight. Hazel Thornton Creswell's father was the prominent businessman John Thornton Creswell, who for thirty-five years was secretary of the SA Cricket Association. Hazel married Ralph in 1909, when she was aged twenty-two and he was twenty-nine. Hazel's untimely death occurred soon after the birth of their third son Malcolm, my father's younger brother. Ralph and Hazel had three sons, christened John Creswell, Basil Creswell (my father) and Malcolm Creswell. The evidence indicates that her death was unexpected and a dreadful blow for Ralph, affecting his life enormously.

Ralph's eldest brother Henry wrote about Hazel to his mother on 25 November 1915, during the First World War:

> And now comes the news of poor Hazel's death. It will be a terrible blow to poor Ralph. I suppose the Creswells will help with the children. Being in the country will make the loss seem all the greater [Ralph was sheep farming at Hansborough in the lower north of SA]. Ralph I know will feel terribly sorry that Dr Wilson was not there to look after Hazel. Those beastly Germans are directly and indirectly responsible for a great deal. [Perhaps the Dr Wilson referred to was in Europe during the First World War.]

In a letter written by Henry to his father from Anzac Cove and dated 7 December 1915 he expresses sympathy for Ralph: 'I hope that time to some extent is soothing Ralph's grief. He must be putting in a very lonely time there'. [Ralph was still at Hansborough.]

A further letter from Henry to his mother, dated 12 January 1916, indicates that Ralph travelled overseas, including to Ceylon, as a distraction from his tragic situation:

> Quite by chance Jack Creswell blew in this morning in charge of some patient. He told me that he had had a letter from his sister Jean [my great aunt and godmother] which she said that Ralph was much better and was taking an interest in everything. Colombo would certainly be a good place for diversion. I hope he went right inland and saw the big rubber plantations.

I interviewed my Uncle Malcolm, Ralph's youngest son, in 2004, when he was nearly ninety years old in an attempt to discover more about Ralph and before I had contemplated compiling this book. In retrospect, I realise I should have asked more penetrating questions! He described Ralph as a 'shadowy figure' in his childhood life, which for him and his two older brothers had not been a happy one. Uncle Malcolm qualified what he had to say about his father, but given the lack of other information about him, I consider it appropriate to include some of his comments:

> Dad started his working life in South Africa as an industrial chemist. He had been to the School of Mines and got the appropriate qualifications. He then went to Johannesburg and worked in the gold mines, or whatever mines there were in Johannesburg – I was never very clear about this. I guess he saved some money then, as he was not married. When he returned to Australia, he bought a small sheep farm near Kapunda, at Hansborough … That's where he set up when he came back to SA and I think he probably married our mother and took her to live at Hansborough. I am a little vague about this … For some reason that is not clear to me, he gave away the Hansborough idea and bought the block at Watervale.

The Hansborough purchase by Ralph has always been somewhat intriguing. Uncle Malcolm told me that he and his wife went searching many years ago for some clues about it and were not successful. While I was researching this book, I decided that my two sisters and I would undertake some investigation as well. What we found was both fortuitous and surprising.

The highway to Eudunda (now called the Thiele Highway) has a signpost pointing westerly from it towards Hansborough, which I suspect is where my uncle Malcolm would have looked for information about his father. Given that the Hansborough railway siding was on that side of the highway (although the railway track had been pulled up at least thirty years ago), it would have made sense to look on that side. On our reconnaissance in 2016, however, we discovered that the Hansborough region was both westerly and easterly of the Thiele Highway.

Once we had discovered this important fact, we took a road heading easterly to a property called Ben Lomond. We then found ourselves, astonishingly, on a public thoroughfare called Newland Road. We then discovered through enquiry that the current owner of Ben Lomond, a Chris Abel, with whom I had previously had some dealings, knew of the past Newland ownership and promised to send me further detail. From a copy of a 1928 pastoral review he had in his possession, he sent the following:

> Ben Lomond is a beautiful stretch of undulating hill country and lies about 65 miles north of Adelaide and eleven miles past the town of Kapunda, with Hansborough siding about one and a half miles away. The property comprises an area of 5681 acres of freehold and was originally part of the Anlaby estate. It was taken up by Sir Richard Butler in 1900 in conjunction with the late Mr Simpson Newland CMG. Both these gentlemen rendered great

> service to the State as Cabinet Ministers and the latter was also well known as the author of that notable book 'Paving the Way'.
>
> The partnership ceased in 1905, and Sir Richard Butler took over the southern half of the property. He later acquired an additional 3000 acres of Anlaby country. In 1919, Mr Guy Butler purchased the northern portion embracing 2100 acres of the original estate from Mr R.D. Newland, and in 1923 acquired that part held by his father, thus regaining the whole 8200 acres.

It appears that Ralph and his first wife Hazel began their married life at Hansborough, where he worked as a sheep farmer, and this is where they initially lived with their three sons. While no records are held by the family, it seems likely that Ralph sold his Hansborough property not long after Hazel died. It may well be that his memories of his early married life with the children were more than he could bear.

It is interesting to reflect that, of all of Simpson and Jane's sons, Ralph was the only one who seemed to have elected to become a pastoralist like his father before him. Sadly, it just did not work out for him. Had Hazel had not died so young, I wonder what Ralph might have done in the future.

It is unclear whether he and Hazel ever lived at Ralph's second property at Watervale, a horticultural block of about seventy acres, which also had an impressive two-storeyed stone house, which still stands. This seems unlikely, given that she died so young, and Ralph's move may have been prompted by her death. There is some poignancy in this, particularly given what emerged later, as Uncle Malcolm's continuing recollections indicate. Uncle Malcolm was largely brought up by Hazel's sister Jean (née Creswell) before being sent boarding school at St Peter's College: Malcolm recounts further:

I think he spent 4 to 5 years in South Africa before returning to SA and marrying [Hazel] at a relatively young age. I'm not sure when he moved to Watervale, as Watervale was the only place I knew. I think he was making his way quite well at Watervale. To my untutored mind as a child, when he used to come down from Watervale, he appeared to be reasonably well off. When he came down, he regularly used to take us all out to lunch and there never seemed to be any shortage of money up until the Depression. When the Depression came along, that wrecked everything for him and lots of other people. I think his income must have fallen almost to zero, because you could not sell the crops. I used to stand out on the main road and sell apricots by the case for about 3 to 4 shillings. It was a big deal if we got 4 shillings. Things were very, very tight and I know he had a very tough time.

This state of affairs brings in sorts of things, as it was about this time that Mildred Dinning appeared on the scene. Mildred was the young nurse who had looked after Dad [Ralph] in Ru Rua Hospital in Barton Tce, North Adelaide. This was a reasonably big and up-market private hospital. I am a little vague about this, but I think Uncle Hal [Sir Henry Newland] was a part-owner or something like that. Dad had a private room there for what seemed like months – it certainly was a pretty long time. Mildred nursed him there, as an employee of the hospital. She had trained there and was a Sister.

I'm not sure of the length of time he was there, but ultimately, Dad was allowed to go home [to Watervale], providing he had a trained nurse to look after him. So the arrangement was that Mildred was to come to Watervale to take up residence. So that is what happened and she came along with considerable excitement. She was a very attractive girl in her early twenties or possibly 25 years old. She first came in the Christmas holidays, so I was in residence at Watervale. I don't know how the marriage to Dad all came about – whether it was in the context of respectability given the times, I could not say. They seemed to get on pretty well together, so I think it was more than just making things respectable.

So she came to live at Watervale to look after Dad because he really was not terribly well. I was never very clear as to what was wrong with him, I have to say. However, I remember when I was at Medical School, Dr De Crespigny saying that he had a peculiar case of an elderly man who was grossly jaundiced, had liver disease and also kidney trouble. I'm sure old 'Crep' didn't realise this might be of particular interest to one of his students, but it all seemed to fit Dad's condition. He talked about this case in a lecture, using it as an example of something he was talking about. I acknowledge that I may have been wrong, but there were at least similarities.

I probably was not old enough to accurately assess the situation but looking back on it, I think Basil [Malcolm's immediate older brother and my father] fell for Mildred and so did I up to a point, although I was considerably more juvenile. But then everything started to go sour and I was not quite sure why. I was very much under Basil's influence and he refused to stay in the house. Something pretty funny went on and I did not know what it was. He took me with him and we built a little humpy out among the apricot trees. We lived there and cooked our own meals and Dad and Mildred lived up in the main house, which was a pretty peculiar situation. That went on for 2 months through the long holidays. At the end of the holidays, I probably went back to school. At that stage, Basil was riding his hunter Anchoosa or whatever its name was, up around the lower north.

I sort of lost track of him at this time. I can't remember how long Dad and Mildred were married, but it was for quite a significant time.

I don't think Basil and Mildred had any sort of affair as he was still pretty young then and she was quite a bit older. I don't know what they were up to, but I think it was probably pie-in-sky. Maybe I was totally wrong because it really has only come to me in the last 20 to 30 years that Basil really had fallen for Mildred – I'm sure he had. Her people came from Mundulla, a little town just out of Bordertown in the South East [of South Australia].

After Dad died, a manager moved in to run the Watervale property; this was when I was at medical school in my first year. His death was no surprise as he had been ill for so long. But I was very immature then and just accepted everything that came along. It was a fairly abnormal family situation.

Looking back to those times, there were fairly marked class distinctions and Dad was a fairly public spirited citizen and, like old Mr Castine across the road, would have been regarded as fairly upper class. They were more or less 'country squire' types, fairly well up the social scale. There were quite a lot of labouring types in the district and Dad employed 2 men until things got tough and then he had one man.

Some sort of rapprochement between Ralph the father and Basil the middle son must eventually have taken place, as the family has a photograph of the Watervale Cricket XI as Premiers of the Mid-North Cricket Association in 1931–32. Ralph is the coach and Basil is the captain of the team. For him to have taken on such a role despite his ill health, means that Ralph's interest in cricket had either revived or continued after Hazel's death. Admittedly, he does not look happy in the photo, but neither do other people in the picture! In typical country style, this photograph, along with a collection of sporting memorabilia, is – or certainly was up till a couple of years or so ago – proudly on display in the front bar of the Watervale Hotel.

The Mildred Dinning part of Ralph's life is somewhat mysterious and I have been fortunate to have acquired a little information about her from her Dinning relatives. Mildred was born on 4 March 1903 and married Ralph on 26 July 1930. She was twenty-seven years old and Ralph was fifty years old. The twenty-three-year age difference is a large one and the details of her life after Ralph's death on 20 September 1933 until her death on 9 March 1965 are scant. Ralph's death certificate records his cause of death as cirrhosis of the liver and chronic nephritis, so it must have been a difficult two to three years.

My Uncle Malcolm recounted the day on which he was married, on 3 February 1940, at the St Peter's College chapel in the afternoon. My father was married on the same day in the same chapel, but in the morning. According to Malcolm, Mildred came to the chapel between the two weddings. She offered Malcolm five pounds as a wedding present, a great deal of money in those days. Whether she offered the same to my father is not known. When I interviewed him, Malcolm told me that he had refused her generosity, to his subsequent regret.

It is also something of a mystery why Ralph had relatively little to do with his children, considering the involvement most of his brothers had with their children and given the tragic, albeit unusual, family circumstances. It is very clear that Ralph was quite unwell for about seven years, after which he died in relatively impecunious circumstances at fifty-three years of age. He had lost many family members, an older brother Phil in 1915 and another brother Clive in 1919, both in unusual circumstances and the latter in a horrific way. The death of his father followed in 1925, and in 1928 his young wife, of whom he seemed to be very fond, also died tragically. Life at Watervale, dealing with the effects of the 1929 Depression, would have been another stressful time. Ralph's eventual second marriage to Mildred Dinning seems to be understandable and a perhaps a good idea at the time. Whether that decision introduced further tensions in his relationship with his children is no more than speculation on my part. Furthermore, a letter from Ralph's father, Simpson, to his eldest son, Henry, dated 23 June 1898 (although unfortunately some text is unreadable), does raise the question of whether Ralph, who was aged eighteen at the time, was not as robust as his older brothers:

> I am glad to say Ralph has recovered & is back at work with Fultons. He does not look to have enough flesh for a young fellow but I hope he will gradually ... harder ... the work easier. No doubt he tried to do too much for his strength, consequently has had to give up La crosse [sic] & games in the dinner hour.

To my considerable regret, and I suspect that of my sisters and first cousins, our paternal grandfather Ralph Dimock remains something of an enigma. This situation is unlikely to change as there is no one alive who can tell us more, nor is there is other known correspondence, apart from that used to compile this relatively short chapter. The description 'shadowy figure' is thus an apt one, albeit a sad and slightly negative and possibly unjust assessment. We will never know for sure.

Epilogue

Each of the five sons of Simpson and Jane had a story to tell. It is fair to assume that the values they inherited and probably had 'thrust upon them' through education and their particular circumstances made them what they were, for better or for worse. Their combined story, untold until now, adds some new information about each of them. The story of their lives, in war and peace and in sport and politics, as they made their respective ways in society, contains a great deal of interesting historical (and personal) detail, which, in my opinion, has the potential to entertain and enlighten more than merely family members. I hope that my wife, sisters, sons, cousins and their children and others in the wider community gain something from the contents of this book, as it has not been assembled purely for family benefit. I can only speculate on its future and its future readers.

Compiling the account in this book has taught me much about my predecessors. I hope that they are not turning in their respective graves as a result of my research into the public and private lives of some of them, examining them over the past several years in ways that I suspect none of them would have imagined would ever occur. I hope I have not included information that one or more of them would prefer not be known, and, just as importantly, I hope I have not missed something important – a real possibility, because of a lack of adequate information about some and the often extraordinary lives of others.

It is a relief for me to have completed a task I set out to do largely because of my own somewhat mysterious grandfather. Along the way I have discovered a considerable amount of interesting information about long-dead relatives in general and certain individuals in particular. I was always in danger of never finishing this account because of the real possibility of new information emerging. For example, after I had done much of the research, I discovered something that none of my relatives or I knew anything about – that Simpson and particularly Victor had given ethnographic material to the South Australian Museum. The material provided by Victor, and probably Leslie Tarlton, forms the basis of the mounted African animal collection on display on the ground floor of the museum.

Of even more interest are the nearly one hundred historic ethnographic items from various parts of Africa also donated to the museum by Victor. Most of these items are now being catalogued, but are yet to be displayed. It is possible that this comprehensive collection of artefacts is one of the earliest from Eastern Africa, and I am continuing to discover more about the collection from museum staff. Discussions are well advanced on the task of digitising and identifying the collection, with the help of Mr Donald Young of Kenya, who is current owner of Newland Tarlton Co. It is my hope that the South Australian Museum and the Nairobi Museum will collaborate on such a collection to the advantage of both institutions and to the international community. It is also my earnest wish that the various indigenous groups in Africa from whence these artefacts originated will also gain some benefit from them.

Although apologies to the dead are not possible, I nevertheless offer, if I have omitted something important or recorded something inappropriate, a posthumous apology here.

Nicholas Paul Newland, AM
Adelaide
March 2018

Notes

1 Kenneth Peake-Jones, *The Branch Without A Tree 1885 to 1985*, RGSSA, 1985. In 1997 the name of the Royal Geographical Society of Australasia, South Australian Branch, was changed to Royal Geographical Society of South Australia.
2 Margaret Black, 'Visit to Undelcarra', Burnside Historical Society, 1982.
3 Published in London by Sampson Low, Son and Marston.
4 Published in 1884 by E.S. Wigg and Son, SA, and Sampson Low, Marston, Searle and Rivington, London.
5 Published by Sampson, Low, Marston & Co Ltd; vol. 1, chapter II.
6 Published by Sampson Low, Marsden, Searle and Rivington.
7 Murray–Darling Basin Authority, Canberra, 2015, p. 11.
8 *The Northern Territory Pastoral Industry 1863–1910*, Melbourne University Press, 1967.
9 In the possession of the author's cousin Helena.
10 This hand-written journal is currently in the possession of his granddaughter Leonie Matheson, who kindly lent it to me, along with Victor's letters, which have been transcribed with her willing and kind consent.
11 Published by Granta books, London.
12 She has been helpful and generous in providing letters and other material for this book.
13 *Henry Simpson Newland* was published by Griffin Press.

Also in this series

Ashton's Hotel: The journal of William Baker Ashton, first governor of the Adelaide Gaol
Rhondda Harris

Behind the Wall: The Women of the Destitute Asylum Adelaide, 1852–1918
Mary Geyer

Bert Edwards
Patricia Sumerling

A Case to Answer: The story of Australia's first European war crimes prosecution
David Bevan

Colonialism and its Aftermath: A history of Aboriginal South Australia
Peggy Brock and Tom Gara (eds)

Emigrants and Historians: Essays in honour of Eric Richards
Philip Payton

The First Wave: Exploring early coastal contact history in Australia
Gillian Dooley, Danielle Clode (eds)

F.J. Gillen's First Diary 1875
Robert S. Gillen (ed.)

Foundational Fictions in South Australian History
Carolyn Collins and Paul Sendziuk (eds)

In Her Own Name: A History of Women in South Australia from 1836
Helen Jones

In the Land of the Magic Pudding: A gastronomic miscellany
Barbara Santich (ed.)

Irish South Australia: New histories and insights
Susan Arthure, Fidelma Breen, Stephanie James, Dymphna Lonergan (eds)

The Last Protector: The illegal removal of Aboriginal children from their parents in South Australia
Cameron Raynes

Mary Lee: The life and times of a 'turbulent anarchist' and her battle for women's rights
Denise George

Miss Marryat's Circle: A not so distant past
Cheryl Williss

One Common Enemy: The *Laconia* Incident: A survivor's memoir
Jim Mcloughlin with David Gibb

Pens and Bayonets: Letters from the Front by soldiers of Yorke Peninsula during the Great War
Don Longo

Searching for the Spirit: Theosophy in Australia, 1879–1939
Jill Roe

South Australia on the Eve of War
Melanie Oppenheimer, Margaret Anderson, Mandy Paul (eds)

Turning Points: Chapters in South Australian history
Robert Foster, Paul Sendziuk (eds)

Yura and Udnyu: A history of the Adnyamathanha of the North Flinders Ranges
Peggy Brock

Wakefield Press is an independent publishing and distribution company based in Adelaide, South Australia.
We love good stories and publish beautiful books.
To see our full range of books, please visit our website at
www.wakefieldpress.com.au
where all titles are available for purchase.
To keep up with our latest releases, news and events, subscribe to our monthly newsletter.

Find us!

Facebook: www.facebook.com/wakefield.press
Twitter: www.twitter.com/wakefieldpress
Instagram: www.instagram.com/wakefieldpress

Printed in Australia
AUHW010801171120
337090AU00007B/7

9 781743 057056